"KEEP FIRING, KEEP FIRING."

It was Blue. He was standing about ten feet behind me, directing the platoon's fire, in full view of the enemy.

I heard a roar over to my left and saw a huge explosion just down the hill, with bodies flying in every direction. Leroy Terry had gotten off a rocket. Meanwhile, Manilla, who still had the use of his right side, was firing his M-16. There were so many bullets whining around me by then that I wasn't sure I'd survive to get off another burst. But North was still standing tall behind me, shouting out orders, so I figured I had no real complaints.

I popped up and began firing again. "My God," the guy next to me screamed. "I'm blind!"

Then about forty yards in front of me, I saw a huge orange flame. I looked back just in time to see Blue crumple and pitch forward. A rocket. The blast had knocked the lieutenant unconscious, and he lay about four feet away, bullets flying all around.

"THE PRIVILEGE OF SERVING WITH THE BRAVE YOUNG MEN WHO WERE BLUE'S BASTARDS MADE THE HARDSHIP AND HORROR OF VIETNAM TOLERABLE. RANDY HERROD WAS ONE OF THEM— AND I WAS ONE OF THEIRS."

—Lt. Col. Oliver North, USMC Ret.

BLUE'S BASTARDS

a true story of valor under fire

RANDY HERROD

A DELL BOOK

Published by
Dell Publishing
a division of
Bantam Doubleday Dell Publishing Group, Inc.
666 Fifth Avenue
New York, New York 10103

ISBN: 0-440-20822-X

Interior design by Jeremiah B. Lighter

Reprinted by arrangement with Regnery Gateway,
Washington, D. C.

Printed in the United States of America

Published simultaneously in Canada

June 1991

10 9 8 7 6 5 4 3 2 1

RAD

TO ALL MEMBERS OF
BLUE'S BASTARDS
LIVING AND DEAD.

ACKNOWLEDGMENTS

I would like to express my gratitude for the editorial assistance of Thomas H. Landess, Al Zuckerman, and Harry Crocker in the preparation of this manuscript.

A NOTE ON SOURCES

Because no official transcript of my trial now exists, I have had to rely principally on my own memory to reconstruct this account, though I have checked my recollections with a few surviving newspaper reports. However, because these events constituted the most psychologically intense experience of my life, I am convinced that what I have written is essentially accurate in every respect, though I will remind the reader that the first person narrator is by definition fallible to some degree.

CONTENTS

BNG

As our commercial jet nosed down toward Saigon airport, I studied the landscape below. At thirty thousand feet it looked green and untroubled, like a travel poster for some tropical hideaway. If you stared hard enough at the intersection of blue sky and treetops, you could almost make yourself believe that you were off on a two-week holiday, that in an hour you'd be stripped down to your trunks, lying on a towel with a pink drink in your hand.

Then we went into a steep bank, and out of the corner of my eye I saw an orange bloom rise out of the jungle and then turn into a black billow of smoke. A shape glinted above the treetops and soared into the sky. I had never seen such a sight before, but somehow I knew what it was: a Phantom jet dropping napalm on the surrounding countryside. Not what you were accustomed to seeing out the window of a commercial flight, particularly as you were making your approach to the airport. Suddenly I found myself wondering, "What in the hell am I doing here?"

But I knew the answer. I had volunteered to come. I was a Marine by choice. Everything that had happened at boot camp had been preparation for this particular moment. When we were learning to fire weapons, to defend ourselves in hand-to-hand combat, to kill the enemy, our drill instructors had told us a hundred times, "Now when you get to Vietnam . . ." No one ever said, "if."

And we'd heard all about the horror from veterans who had returned from the slaughter to train their own replacements. For example, I knew that the average life of a gunner in a firefight was three to seven seconds, that as soon as the enemy spotted a machine gun in action, they'd concentrate their fire on that area. I knew these things because I was a gunner.

But as we touched down on the runway at Saigon, I wasn't thinking about that particular statistic. I was worried about which unit I'd be joining, and more specifically, whether or not I'd be assigned to the 9th Marines. We'd all talked about it on the flight over, and you could tell by what people said that they were plenty scared. The 9th Marines were known as "the Walking Dead," because in effect their lives were over. You were either "medevacked" out or shipped home in a body bag. So if you were assigned there, you could just about write your goodbye letters the day you arrived.

As we walked around in the airport, stretching our legs after the long flight, we talked about other things; but when a sergeant came for us, we immediately grew silent.

"Okay. All you BNGs line up here while I call the roster," the sergeant shouted.

"What's a BNG?" somebody called out.

The sergeant looked up without smiling.

"A BNG is a brand new guy."

Then he told us we would all be loaded onto

a C130 and flown to Da Nang, where we would receive our unit assignments. So the suspense would be postponed for a while, though not for long, since the flight to Da Nang took less than an hour. We had talked constantly to one another all the way across the Pacific Ocean, but now the plane was silent, except for the roar of the prop engines. I figured everyone was thinking about the 9th Marines, just as I was. I had not prayed in a while, but I began to pray again on that last leg to Da Nang.

When we got off the plane we were met by trucks and hauled directly to the processing center, a huge compound that serviced both incoming and outgoing men, just across the road from Freedom Hill, one of the largest R-and-R centers in Vietnam. I sat down on one of the hard rows of bleachers along with the rest of the BNGs. Soon we would know, one way or the other.

A lance corporal with a clipboard stepped forward and began to read the names and unit assignments—slowly, matter-of-factly. And one by one I counted the number going to the 9th Marines. Barnes and McKee, both of whom had been with me in boot camp. Kitchener and Morrison, whom I saw over my shoulder, both hunched over, staring at the floor. I should have felt sorry for them, but I was too busy praying, "Oh God, please don't send me there!"

"Herrod, Private Randall D."

I stopped breathing.

"Company Kilo, 3rd Battalion."

I breathed again. I had dodged my first bullet in Vietnam. But the day's terror wasn't quite over.

"You'll be leaving for your units tomorrow

morning," the lance corporal said, after he'd read the last name. Then he led us down the dirt street to a two-story barracks and told us we'd be spending the night there.

"But don't sleep too soundly," he said with a thin smile, "because the Vietcong drop rockets on Da Nang about every two hours."

As I lay in my bunk that night, all my senses alert, not knowing whether I'd wake up in the morning, I thought about staging battalion at Camp Pendleton, crawling under barbed wire with machine gun bullets whining overhead, my eardrums assaulted by exploding sticks of TNT, sloshing through snake-infested creeks and rivers; and I realized that nothing in my life to date —not even my Marine training—had prepared me for what I was going through now. I figured everybody else was going through the same agony, so I kept my mouth shut and tried not to think too much. One by one they began to fall asleep. I could hear their heavier breathing, and finally I fell asleep too, having concluded that the lance corporal was just giving us a hard time because we were BNGs.

About 2:30 in the morning all hell broke loose. The whole building rattled with the explosion and I sat up in bed to see the sky lit up like it was daytime. And it didn't stop with that first blast. They came one after another—the explosions and the white flashes, worse than the worst electric storm I'd ever been through. We lay there in silence, too scared even to talk, expecting the next one to blow the barracks into a million pieces. We were certain that every rocket was exploding in the street just outside, but we learned the next morning that they were really landing about a mile away.

Then, just as suddenly as the barrage had begun, it ceased; and there was silence and darkness. But none of us could go back to sleep; and sure enough, in about two hours they hit us again, and we lived through another half hour of bombardment. Finally the sky lightened, then turned to blue, and it was day again. We had made it through our first night in Vietnam. When I looked at my face in the mirror I saw strain and fear. But after I'd washed and shaved, I was all guns, guts, and glory again.

After chow we piled into trucks and headed up to Quang Tri. I was dropped off at Kilo Company headquarters, found my way to the duty hut, reported, and handed over my orders. A gunnery sergeant named Banna happened to be in the hut, and he told me I would be a replacement in the 2nd Platoon.

"They were chosen Honor Platoon for the changing of command back at 3rd Marine Division Headquarters," he said. "They won't be back for a couple of days."

He grinned. "You're lucky."

I was sent to my squad tent, where I dumped my gear on the first empty cot I saw. Then I fell on the unmade "rubber bitch," and slept till late afternoon, my dreams uninterrupted by explosions. I woke up in time for chow, and while I was in the mess hall, talking to a couple of guys, I found out a little bit about my new outfit.

"They're called Blue's Bastards," one of them said.

I looked puzzled.

"In the brevity code 'blue' means 'north.'"
"I still don't get it," I said.
They laughed, but gave no explanation.
"You'll find out soon enough."

Two days later I found out. I was over in another platoon, talking to a couple of guys, when someone stuck his head in the tent and yelled, "Herrod, go to the duty hut. Your platoon leader's waiting for you."

When I came into the hut I saw him standing there, dressed in camouflage utilities and black boots that glittered with a high gloss. As he offered his hand I noticed that though it was still midmorning and he'd just shaved a few hours ago, he already had five o'clock shadow.

"I'm Lieutenant Oliver North," he said. "I'm leader of the 2nd Platoon."

From the moment I met him I had the feeling that he was about my height and was looking me straight in the eye. It wasn't until years later that I saw a photograph of him standing next to me and realized that he was only about six feet—four inches shorter than I was. There's a quality about some men that can add several inches to their height, and North had it, even that first day. It was in his eyes: They burned with a bright light. It was in his voice and the way he carried himself. You knew you took orders from this man. You didn't have to see the bars.

He told me a little bit about the platoon, the guys on my gun team, the things we'd be doing. We were a kind of troubleshooting outfit, one that would often be sent in when somebody else had run into bad trouble. The men were all good

Marines, he said. In fact, they were the best in
the division, as everybody knew; and I would
have to learn from them and do what they said
until I got my bearings. Then he told me to follow him and he'd take me to meet some of the
others.

As big as I was, I was half in awe of him
when I left the duty hut, but I realized I was
feeling something else as well. I hadn't joined
the Marines to die. I'd expected to fight, survive,
and go back in one piece when my tour was
over. But for the last few hours I'd been scared.
Now I was more confident. For the first time
since we'd circled the Saigon airport, I felt like I
had a chance with this man leading me.

I followed North ("Blue"—now I understood) back to the platoon area, where I met the
gun team I'd be joining. There were two of them
waiting for me. North introduced us and then
left.

Romeo Rodriguez was the team leader, a
wiry Puerto Rican from San Antonio, Texas. He
spoke with an accent that was half-Spanish, half-
Southwestern, and seemed easygoing, though he
looked tough. I found out later that he had a
great sense of humor and made a joke out of
everything we did, particularly when it was dangerous or unpleasant. So he was a good team
leader.

Al Manilla, an Italian-American from New
York City, was stockier and had a cocky tilt to
his head. From the beginning his attitude
seemed to say: "Here I am. If you like me, fine. If
you don't, then you can go to hell." Manilla likewise had a sense of humor, but it was off-beat.
He would laugh at things that no one else

laughed at; and then, when someone would tell a particularly funny joke, he would sit stony-faced while the rest of us broke up.

We sat on Manilla's bunk and talked for a while. We didn't get down to business at first. We just shot the breeze about where we'd come from, boot camp, what was going on in the world. Then we went to chow. Everybody seemed so relaxed I thought we might not be going into the field for a while; but when we got back to the tents, one of the guys told us that the word had come down, that we'd be moving out the next morning.

I brought my gear over and Rodriguez showed me how to get it all into my backpack.

"You have to do it just right," he said. "Otherwise you'll be hauling around half your stuff under your arms. And no ammunition belts around your chest. Blue's orders. The ammunition gets dirty and then it malfunctions."

It never occurred to me that I could get everything into that small backpack—my personal stuff, C-rations, mess gear, the whole works. But Romeo showed me; and when he was through—sure enough, it was all in there.

Then he explained how the machine gun team operated.

"The gunner and the A-gunner fire the machine gun. The team leader directs the fire. You and Al will be in one foxhole. I'll be in another. I'll spot the targets and fire at them first. I carry an M-16 rifle and every fifth round is a tracer. You'll be able to watch the tracers and know where to concentrate your fire."

"I thought there were four men on a machine gun team. Who's the fourth?"

"You're the third *and* fourth," he said. "You'll be A-gunner and ammo humper. The A-gunner feeds the ammo into the gun while it's firing. The ammo humper carries the ammunition."

Then he showed me how the gun operated and how to clean it.

"That's all there is to know," he said. "When the shooting starts, it'll take you a few minutes to get the hang of it. Then you'll be an expert."

I thought about the lifespan of a gunner in combat—that three to seven seconds—but said nothing.

He took me around to meet the other guys in the tent, and then everybody got down to cleaning weapons and packing gear. A few were writing letters back home. It was a quiet time, with no one saying much to anyone else. Then one of the guys I'd just met brought out his camera and asked us all to come outside while he took our picture.

"Hey, Herrod," he said. "You come too. I don't have you yet."

So I went outside with the rest and stood there, utility cap down over my forehead, brim turned up, while he snapped several pictures. Then we went back inside. A few minutes later I saw guys from another squad tent out for a photography session. Everybody seemed in a light mood, and it took me a while to realize what was going on. This was a time to take pictures of guys you'd been friendly with, because you didn't know who would be coming back and who wouldn't.

In an envelope in the back of my desk drawer I still have a stack of old color photos, most of them taken on days when we were moving out. Some of the grinning faces belong to guys who have been dead almost twenty years now. I've even forgotten a few of their names. But most of them I remember; and while many of the group pictures are of men I hardly knew, I still can't bring myself to throw them away, remembering when and why they were taken.

Late that afternoon—after we'd cleaned our weapons, packed our gear, taken photographs, and written letters home—we had a game of football. Since we didn't have a ball, we made one out of our Marine tube socks—slipping on one sock after another, then pounding the mass with our fists until it took on a shape that vaguely resembled the real thing.

Once the ball was made, we chose up sides and played as if we were in the Orange Bowl, wearing our steel helmets and flak jackets. It was a hard, rough game, with neither side giving any quarter. The blocks and tackles were bone-jarring, and you'd clobber your closest friend if he stood in the way of a touchdown. This is the way Lieutenant North wanted us to play. (The football games before combat had been his idea.)

After the game we went to the mess hall for a last normal meal. When we got into the field we would be eating C-rations heated in the can, if we found time to eat. That night I lay awake again, but not as long as I had in Da Nang when the rockets were exploding outside. I was beginning to feel that I now had some control over whether I lived or died, though the idea of combat still gave me a queasy feeling.

The next morning before dawn, we fell out

in full gear and were driven by truck to a staging area, where we were to be picked up by helicopters. There we went through several rituals that I learned were standard procedure with Blue's Bastards. First, the four squad leaders were issued ammunition, which they passed out to the men. I got eight fully loaded magazines of ammunition for my M-14 rifle; and since I was ammo humper, I got four cans of M-60 machine gun ammo, which weighed about 18 pounds per can.

Then, as we climbed into the copters, we were again inspected by Lieutenant North, who checked to see that we had the required amount of ammunition and that it was properly packed. For example, he made certain that hand grenades were deep inside the pockets of our flak jackets rather than hanging on the outside. Too many Marines had been lost early in the war because a pin had been jerked out by a branch or vine while some guy was plowing through the jungle like John Wayne.

I noticed North spent a little extra time looking me over before he moved me on into the copter, but I had no resentment. I was beginning to understand that because he ran a tight ship, I probably had a better chance of surviving. In fact, something Romeo had told me at chow began to make sense. Ordinarily, when men were about to be rotated they were taken off the front line and returned to Da Nang or Saigon. But North's men would ask to remain in combat with him till the very end, not because they were gung ho but because they knew they were less likely to get killed that way.

We were flown to the edge of the bush, and

from there we had to move through rough terrain on foot, fighting nature and our own physical limitations. My first day in the bush was rough. The temperature was around 115 degrees in the shade, and I had everything I owned packed on my back: my M-14 rifle, eight magazines of 308 ammunition, those four cans of M-60 machine gun ammo, my clothes, four water-filled canteens, and 21 cans of C-ration meals. By the end of the day, when we finally came out of the bush, insect-bitten and bleeding from vines and razorlike leaves, I could barely move my arms and shoulders, they ached so. That night I was ready to sleep the sleep of the dead, but I found out soon enough that no one slept too well on patrol in Lieutenant Oliver North's platoon.

Everybody had to take his turn on watch; and since we were a three-man machine gun team, I would have to stand watch every three hours until dawn, listening over the field telephone for any messages from headquarters. When Romeo tried to wake me at 2300 hours (11 P.M.) I was only vaguely aware of him as he shook me.

"Randy," he said finally, handing me the telephone. "It's your girl calling."

I sat up, for a moment believing it was true. He shoved the receiver into my hand, then laughed quietly, rolled over, and was asleep before I could protest.

The next morning when we went on patrol along the back of the ridge, I got my first good look at the landscape of Leatherneck Square. It was like we were on a grassy moon, full of enormous craters made by B-52 bombs. There was still some green scrub brush and elephant grass about five feet high, but much of that had been scorched black by the bombs, and the rest was twisted and humped over, as if a tornado had ripped through it. As I stared, I realized that the craters went on and on and on, as far as the eye could see, over rolling hills and down into hollows. The magnitude of the devastation was awesome. Even as I looked at it, my imagination couldn't keep up with my eyes.

I remember thinking: "Why would anyone want this sorry land? No one could possibly plow it or plant it or build anything on it. Not for a hundred years. So what was all the fighting about?"

As we moved down into the hollows I noticed that trees were also in short supply, though we passed hundreds of charred stumps and branches that you had to walk around or step over. At one time there had been small wooden bridges spanning the streams and creeks, but the bridges too had been blown away, so we had to wade the shallow, flowing water. It felt good to splash across from one bank to the other, but as soon as you stepped onto dry land, you could see the steam rising from your own body as the moisture evaporated in the glare of the sun.

That morning, as the platoon was moving through the ravaged countryside, I realized I was feeling more and more secure. I saw experienced veterans to the front and rear of me, and North was leading the way. He walked with seeming indifference to any danger that might lie ahead, but he was also alert; and every so often he would stop and make a 360-degree sweep of the terrain with his eyes. I had a good feeling about him and began to relax a little. That was a mistake.

After walking about seven clicks (kilometers) we took up a position, dug in, and lit up cigarettes. I sat down by Romeo.

"Is the whole country torn up like this, with nothing but patches of green?"

"No. Soon we'll go up on the ridge. Then we'll be at the DMZ, the 38th parallel—Mutter's Ridge. It's pockmarked like Leatherneck Square, but there's no green stuff at all. It's all been napalmed away. It looks like it's been scraped by a cleaning crew."

"Why that particular place?" I asked.

"Because anytime we go up there, they try to blow us off. Anytime they're up there, we try to blow them off."

"So when will that begin?" I asked.

"More than likely around Happy Hour."

He told me Happy Hour was just before nightfall or right after dawn, when the North Vietnamese usually launched their attacks.

"Do they even know we're here?" I asked.

"They know it."

Though it was still hot, a small breeze sprang up, so I made a pillow of my backpack, stretched out, and tried to relax. At some point, exhausted, my muscles aching, I fell asleep. Suddenly my head seemed to explode. I sat bolt upright and found myself looking into the eyes of Lieutenant Oliver North. It took me a moment to realize he had slapped my helmet as hard as he could.

"Don't you ever go to sleep while we're out on patrol," he said. "Not ever. You understand?"

I nodded groggily.

"Yes, sir," I replied.

"Never," he said evenly. "Now sit up and don't get so comfortable."

I was mad at him for making such a big deal of it and ashamed of myself, but no one else seemed to notice. Gradually, as I thought about it, I realized he'd done it for my own good, and I was able to shake it off. But I never forgot the way it felt to have my helmet clobbered that hard, and I never went to sleep again on patrol.

One thing was certain—I didn't get any sleep that night. Sure enough, at dusk the whole ridge exploded, just as Romeo had said it would; and we were right in the middle of Happy Hour.

Manilla and I manned our gun, ready in case we saw any of the enemy, ready if Romeo, in a neighboring foxhole, began to fire. But for a while all we did was hunch against the ground and pray silently, as orange-white explosions lit up the landscape, rattling the whole ridge and sending slides of dirt pouring into our foxhole. These explosions were louder than anything I'd been through at Da Nang. They were blasting in front of us, behind us, to the right and left. I wondered how long they could go before they dropped one right on our heads.

"It's mortars and artillery fire," said Manilla, who seemed uncomfortable, but not nearly as shaken as I was. "It'll go on for a little while longer. Then Blue will call in an air strike. You'll see some fireworks on the other side of the ridge. And we'll get the hell out."

"Is that what happens every time?"

"Yeah," he said, as if he knew all about it.

And sure enough, after a few minutes more of artillery fire and mortars, somebody cheered somewhere in the darkness, and we heard the Phantom jets overhead. Then the sound of strafing. Suddenly the crest of the ridge looked like it was on fire. Our planes were bombing the North Vietnamese mortar and artillery positions. The artillery fire didn't stop entirely, but it diminished to an occasional round. The gun and mortar crews on the other side of the ridge had their hands full.

Just to our right a figure ran up to Romeo, mumbled something, then scurried back up the ridge. Romeo called over to us.

"Get ready to move out."

When the order came, we didn't need encouragement. We clambered out of the foxhole and half-ran, half-slid down the ridge, crouching to avoid shrapnel and flying debris. Romeo joined us, and then the rest, including Lieutenant North, whose eyes shone even brighter now than they had back at the duty hut in Quang Tri. Still a little wobbly myself, I had the impression that North was almost enjoying himself, that he was in his element.

He looked around, rapidly counting the men present. Then he nodded.

"Let's go home," he said.

Home? Forty-eight hours earlier I wouldn't have used that word to describe Quang Tri; but as we moved away from the ridge, I was glad to be going back there. I was still jumpy, and the exploding shells behind us still sounded loud (though no louder now than the rocket attack back at Da Nang); but I'd been through combat, I hadn't disgraced myself, and I was alive. Also, though I didn't yet think of myself as one of Blue's Bastards, I knew I was no longer a BNG.

BLUE AND THE BASTARDS

AFTER WE CAME down from the ridge we were taken by chopper back down to Vandergriff Combat Base, where we were resupplied and where for a few days we hung around, drank a few cold beers, shot the bull, and one night saw *Barbarella,* a sexy film starring an actress named Jane Fonda, about whom we'd heard very little at the time. During this period I got to know the platoon a lot better, and for the first time I noticed how different we were in many respects. For one thing, we all came from different parts of the country, and some even came from other nations. I was from Oklahoma. Ernie Tuten was from Georgia. Manilla was from New York. Jerry Marchand was from Canada. And a guy whose name I couldn't pronounce was from Indonesia.

Also, we were a mixed bag ethnically and racially. I was half Indian. Our rocket man was black. Rodriguez was Mexican-American. Manilla was Italian-American. And we had the Indonesian as well as an assortment of WASPs. So if you were producing a poster for Brotherhood

Week, you could have photographed our platoon
and had all the ingredients.

But though we were different in a number
of respects, I soon found out that the team spirit
of the platoon made individual differences seem
irrelevant. Individualism is a fine thing in a
democratic society—during normal times. I
come from the Southwest, a part of the country
that has always been strong on personal freedom. In Oklahoma we have as many eccentrics
per square mile as any place in the United
States, and we're proud of them. But anyone
who has studied history knows that a society
fighting for its life often has to curtail individual
freedom in the interest of survival.

A Marine combat unit is by definition a "society fighting for its life."

You can't have a platoon made up of eccentrics who get up every morning and decide
whether or not they're going to fight today. Nor
can you let each man determine just what he's
going to do and when he's going to do it. The
Marine who says, "I did it my way," is lying in a
graveyard surrounded by all his buddies.

So the first thing you look for in a combat
unit is respect for authority—respect for the guy
who gives the orders when you go into combat.
If his men have no confidence in him—if they
think he's stupid or cowardly or foolhardy—
then there's a very good chance they'll screw up,
either because they did something they were
told not to do, or else they didn't do something
they were told to do.

When that happens, people die unnecessar-
ily. That's why the Marines spend so much time
in boot camp destroying the petty egos of en-

listed men and why at Quantico they drive their officers to the breaking point: because when you put these two elements together in the field, you're supposed to end up with a fighting team, not a collection of Rambos.

So when we got back to Vandergriff, I decided to find out what kind of field commander North was. As we were sitting around drinking beer one night, I raised the question.

"Lieutenant North seems like a first-rate officer. Is he for real?"

"He's the best," said Ernie Tuten. "Not just the best in the company or in the Third Marines, but the best anywhere."

Tuten was a gunner like me, though in the other machine gun team. Six feet two, he weighed about 180 pounds and spoke with a Georgia drawl.

"He leads," said Jim Honey in a quiet voice. Honey—a short, dark-haired man—spoke softly and said very little, but like the others, he was dependable in combat.

"What do you mean?" I asked.

"He doesn't tell you what to do," said Honey. "He shows you."

"Notice where he is when we're out in the bush," said Bill Echternkamp. "Always out in front. When you follow him, you do it literally. If we run into trouble, he's right there to take the first round."

Echternkamp reached out for his beer, and I noticed a Marine Corps tattoo on one arm. Six feet tall with brown hair, he looked like a lifer, though it turned out that, like me, he was just in for the one tour.

"He can make inspirational talks when he

has to," Tuten said, "but mainly he's good because he's cool and methodical. He goes by the book."

"But not necessarily the book he studied in Annapolis," said Echternkamp, with a grin.

"No," admitted Tuten. "He's written a few chapters of his own, mainly from what he's learned out here. Notice that we all wear our steel helmets in the field. Guys in other units wear their liners, or sometimes nothing at all on their heads. Blue says he's seen too many sudden attacks where guys ran around without their helmets or lost them because they weren't buckled. Later the same guys were walking around with empty eye sockets and missing foreheads. So we wear our steel helmets at all times when we're in the field."

"We also clean our ammunition as well as our weapons," said Echternkamp.

"What do you mean?" I asked.

"When we come in from the bush, we wipe off each round. Lieutenant's orders. He says that when rounds are grimy, they'll jam a rifle or a machine gun. No one knows which round will stop some gook charging at you. So Blue says to assume it's the one you haven't cleaned. That's why you see guys in our platoon, sitting around, polishing ammunition as if it were the family silver."

"He also makes us bend the pins on our hand grenades so they won't come out too easily," said Honey. "You could lose a whole squad if a pin got snagged on a tree."

"Something else," said Tuten. "He won't let us cut the plates out of our flak jackets, the way guys in the other units do."

"Why not?" I asked. "Those jackets were designed for subfreezing weather. It's usually pretty hot around here, isn't it?"

"In the summer it's around 120 degrees," said Honey.

"That's why most of the guys cut out the plates and go around in nothing more than a glorified T-shirt," said Tuten. "It's more comfortable, but you lose a considerable amount of protection."

"The lieutenant says that the flak jacket is the modern equivalent of medieval armor," said Echternkamp. "It's designed to withstand shrapnel and anything else that's flying around in the air. It could mean the difference between life and death. So if you're one of Blue's Bastards, you wear your flak jacket the way it was issued to you."

"And you catch hell from the guys in the other units," said Tuten.

"But some of the same guys that used to jeer are dead now or armless," said Honey quietly. "And just because they wanted to be a little more comfortable in the hot weather. The same guys that called us Blue's Bastards."

They explained to me that the phrase was invented by outsiders who, watching the platoon do all these things, thought that North was too full of guns-guts-and-glory and that his men were too worshipful. Part of this feeling grew out of their contempt for what they thought was an excessive preoccupation with safety. North hated to lose men more than any other commander in the field. He took it personally every time. Even when it clearly wasn't his fault, he would blame himself. So he was especially attentive to each small detail.

"They called us Blue's Bastards to jeer at us," said Tuten, "but we got to the point where we liked the name and started using it ourselves."

During the course of the evening we were joined by a couple of other guys—Whip Whipple and John Redmon, both of whom I liked immediately. The first thing they told me was what they did in the platoon. I was already learning that this was about the most important thing you could know about a man.

Whipple, I found out, manned the M-79 grenade launcher (the "blooper"). Six feet tall with sandy brown hair, he came from Massachusetts; and he could have been a stand-up comedian. As he drank beer and told me stories about the platoon, I found myself laughing at the grimmest situations. Long treks through the bush, heavy mortar attacks, guys getting killed—Whipple made a good joke out of everything. He had a perfect sense of timing; and after I spent some more time out in the field, I learned how important he was to the morale of the others. He could turn us completely around on those rare occasions when the whole platoon was down. (Somewhere in the bottom of a cardboard box I still have a wire he sent me when I got back to the United States, which reads "Welcome home" and is signed "Blooperman.")

Redmon was a squad leader and like Whipple was six feet tall. Quick to laugh, he told me he was from Kansas City, Missouri, where his father owned a tool-and-die factory.

"Redmon is our platoon scavenger," Whipple said. "He can locate food no matter where the mess sergeant hides it. Got a nose like a rat."

"Yeah," said Tuten. "He keeps us in choice C-rations, if there's such a thing. And he can smell beer when it's still in the can."

I later learned that Redmon's father was rich, so rich that once when John had a week of R-and-R coming, he caught a hop to Honolulu, where his father met him in a private Learjet and took him on to the States. Then, at the end of the week, his father flew him back to Honolulu and dropped him off just in time to catch a flight back to Vietnam.

"Hey, Marchand," Redmon called out. "Come over here and meet Herrod."

Jerry Marchand was Ernie Tuten's machine gun team leader. Just under six feet, with brown hair, he was a Canadian who had joined the Marine Corps to become a U.S. citizen at a time when American kids were going off to Canada and denouncing the country they were born in.

As Marchand made his way toward us, Whipple said, "This guy can walk just like the Pink Panther in the Peter Sellers movie. Hey, Panther, do it!"

Suddenly Marchand, beer in hand, broke into his imitation, and I have never laughed so hard in my life. It was absolutely perfect. In the months to come, when we were lying around with nothing to do except worry about what was going to happen next, someone would always yell out, "Pink Panther!" and Marchand would jump up and give us about thirty seconds of the famous moves. Sometimes he would even do it when we were on a sweep. But never for very

long, because it would crack us up at just the
time when we had to be most quiet and alert.

That night I got to know several of the guys who
would be my buddies for the next few months.
Tuten and I got along particularly well because
we had come from the same part of the country
and because we were both gunners and talked
continually about combat situations and how
we could make the best use of our weaponry.
Following a firefight in which I had been recommended for a decoration, Ernie began calling
me "Ira," after the Marine hero in "The Ballad of
Ira Hayes."

There was more than a little irony in his use
of this name, which the others picked up. Ernie
was as brave as anybody, and more medal-
hungry than most; but though he went through
the same attacks and took the same risks as the
rest of us, somehow he was always at the wrong
place when the heavy action came down. In fact,
I think Ernie Tuten may have been the only man
in the platoon who didn't win the Purple Heart
at least once.

Another guy who came from Georgia and
who became a buddy was Leroy Terry, who
manned the LAW rocket launcher. He was a
huge black man, six-three and about 230
pounds, and nobody ever messed with him.
Quiet and good-natured, he had been a professional wrestler in his hometown of Atlanta,
which may explain how he lost his front teeth.
Whenever he would smile, which was often, he
revealed a huge gap, which must have made it
difficult for him to chew. But it had been his
choice: When he arrived in Vietnam, he had

taken one look at what was going on there and had shipped his expensive bridge back to Georgia for safekeeping.

We called Terry "The Mighty T" long before anyone had heard of "The A Team." He was one of the most powerful men I have ever seen, but slow to anger. When we were in trouble, or were expecting trouble, it was always reassuring to look over to my right and see Leroy towering over the landscape like a redwood. He was also a dead shot with the rocket launcher, which was a new weapon in Vietnam.

Unlike the old "bazooka," the LAW was made up of plastic and was disposable. You fired four or five rockets—as many as you could carry —and then you busted the thing up with your E-tool (folding spade) and made sure it could not be put together again. You did this because the North Vietnamese, using a board, would convert LAW rocket launchers into mortars and use them against Marines. (They would even turn pop bottles into lethal weapons.)

Most of us didn't carry anything as formidable and as deadly as a rocket launcher. Most of the guys were equipped with M-16 rifles, which had selector knobs on them so they could fire either semi-automatically or automatically. M-16s could get off six or eight bursts at a time, just like a machine gun; but they could not do it steadily, since they were magazine-fed. The M-60 machine gun, which was fed by a belt, could fire bursts of eight rounds as long as the ammunition belt was sliding through. If a machine gun didn't jam, it was a beautiful thing to watch.

But when Leroy fired off the rocket

launcher we were all awed. If you handled it properly, you could hit a man in the chest as easily as you could with a rifle. And the back blast was lethal up to a hundred feet.

It's amusing to watch Sylvester Stallone run into a building, stop, and fire a LAW rocket launcher. Anyone who did that inside four walls would be burnt bacon within two seconds. Leroy was very careful how he handled the weapon, and we were likewise careful when he was about to blast off.

There was another Southerner in the platoon, a guy from Louisiana who had a Creole name nobody could pronounce, so we all called him "Frenchy." I got to know Frenchy very well, because we both corresponded with the same girl. Of course, neither one of us knew her very well. I had seen her only once, and Frenchy had never even met her, but she wrote to both of us once a week, and we wrote her almost as often.

Her name was Kay, and I had met her just as I was about to be shipped overseas. I told her where I was going, and then as a joke I said, "Are you going to write to me?"

"Sure," she said, "if you'll write to me first."

I took her address, still half-kidding; but after I had settled down in Kilo Company I sent her a letter, telling her where I was and what it was like in Vietnam. In a couple of weeks I got an answer. I read some of her wisecracks to Frenchy, who was bunking next to me.

"Gee," he said, "I wish I knew a girl who would write me letters like that."

"I hardly know this one," I said, and I told him how it had all happened.

"You suppose she would write to me too?"

"Write her and ask," I said, and threw him the envelope with Kay's return address. He copied it, borrowed some stationery, and started a letter that afternoon. A week or so later he came into the bunker, a big grin on his face, holding an envelope.

From that time on he got as many letters from Kay as I did, and probably wrote a few more. She would send me messages in his letters and vice versa, so we had a lot to talk about in the next few months.

These, then, were the guys I had known and liked from the very beginning. Later, after I had been in the platoon for two or three months, more BNGs joined us as replacements, and I got to know several of them quite well. One was Jim Lynch, a short, stocky New Yorker with black hair who had the same kind of brash and boisterous personality as Manilla. The first time I saw him I knew he was too cocky not to get his comeuppance. It was the second day after his arrival, and I was cleaning the machine gun while Lynch was looking over my shoulder, talking a mile a minute right next to my ear. When he finally began telling me how to do my job, I knew I'd had enough.

"How about going up to Gunny Banna's and getting me a TR Double-E," I told him.

"Who's Banna?" Lynch asked.

"The company gunnery sergeant," I said, and gave him directions.

When he told Gunny he wanted a TR Double-E, Gunny grinned.

"Tell Herrod to chop down his own goddamn tree."

Lynch came back red in the face, but by

then I'd finished cleaning the gun and was ready for a beer.

Bob Mullins came in that same group of replacements, a guy we all liked but were a little nervous about. Mullins was an ammo humper who topped six-two, with blond hair and a complexion that remained milk white no matter how much time he spent in the sun. From Boston, he was a friendly, easygoing guy, with only one fault: he slept too much. Some people under stress become irritable and jumpy. Others eat or drink too much. Mullins would go to sleep. And since we were always under stress, Mullins was always sleeping. In the field we'd see him lying spread-eagle on the sand or draped over the charred stump of a tree, oblivious to what was going on around him. For a long while we laughed. Then one night it was no longer funny.

There were many other members of Blue's Bastards, but these were the ones I knew best, the ones I most remember. In looking back over the roster, I can see for the first time how much alike we were, not only in physical stature but also in personality and general outlook. It was as if we were all made from a cookie mold—and in a sense we were. After all, Lieutenant North screened us at the beginning and made certain that no one of a different stripe stayed in the 2nd Platoon.

I suppose the typical description of one of Blue's Bastards would read as follows:

HEIGHT: between six and six-
                   three;

WEIGHT:	160 to 180 pounds;
AGE:	around 19 years old;
DISPOSITION:	casygoing; quick to smile; not given to moodiness or depression;
ATTITUDE:	full of guns, guts, and glory; eager to go into combat; easy to wound; almost impossible to kill; responds quickly and without question to orders while in combat; spends free time drinking beer and talking about ways to kill the enemy; extremely patriotic and confused by the anti-war movement; doesn't smoke or shoot dope; wonders what will replace the "high" of a firefight back in civilian life.

This typical profile would have described most of us to a T and all of us to some degree, even Lieutcnant North himself. But it would be a mistake to say that he made us the way we were. We were born that way, and natural selectivity brought us to that particular outfit under that particular junior officer. We were Marines by choice. We were sent to Vietnam because all good Marines were sent there during the late

1960s. And we got into North's platoon because he wanted men like us—and no other kind.

But if he didn't make us into the men we were, he certainly brought out what was already there. When he talked to us, we listened, because he was saying things we could understand and respond to. He knew our language, the words and phrases that would appeal to us and move us to think and act as a coherent fighting force. We were confident that he thought and felt exactly as we did, so we trusted his instincts as well as we trusted our own—and maybe more so.

You must remember that in World War II the average fighting man was 27 years old, while in Vietnam the average age was 19—about what it ran for our platoon. North, on the other hand, was 24, had been to Annapolis, and as a consequence knew more than we did. We thought of him as an older brother rather than as an equal who happened to have bars on his shoulders. We looked up to him, went to him for advice, and listened when he talked. We also jumped when he gave an order, and I don't think there was a man in the outfit who ever doubted his ability to command.

In turn, he took a heavy burden on his shoulders for each one of us. I don't know what it says in the *Officer's Manual* about the factors a platoon leader should consider in evaluating the morale of his men, but I'll bet that Blue covered them all—and then some. He would come around periodically and talk to each one of us, sometimes in private, sometimes in groups of two and three. There was never anything formal about these sessions. They seemed to come about by accident. But while he was shooting the breeze he would ask us about news from home, about how we were getting along with the other men in the outfit, about specific problems we were experiencing, particularly concerning combat.

From time to time most of us would admit that we were afraid, and once in a while someone would go through a particularly bad period and talk to Blue on his own. The lieutenant was always quick to point out that he too was afraid, that everybody felt fear from time to time, that it was nothing to worry about—provided you didn't let yourself think about it too much. His admission and reassurances were always enough to quiet our nerves, and we never had any real morale problems in the 2nd Platoon.

Our respect for North and his continuing concern for us paid big dividends in the field. Though we were under enemy fire more times than I can remember, and though all of us (with the exception of Ernie Tuten) were wounded from time to time, we only lost one of the Bastards during the more than six months I served in the unit, and that death was unavoidable, the result of a direct hit by mortar fire rather than a mistake or somebody's fault. I can't help feeling that our low death rate was the result of discipline and loyalty rather than luck. Furthermore, I'm convinced that the high losses in other units throughout Vietnam can be explained in part by a lack of these qualities.

The period of the 1960s was one of self-centered individualism. And though the most rebellious young people avoided the service by hiding out in Canada or simply by not registering for the draft, most guys who went into the armed services—and even into the Marine Corps—were inevitably touched by the spirit of the times. So in Vietnam you saw it all: alcoholism, dope, lax discipline, and a certain amount of out-and-out insubordination. But not in our platoon. It was as if we were bypassed by the virus that infected the rest of our generation and were left the way our fathers had been 25 years earlier.

I'm aware that this description is to some degree self-serving, and there will be those who resent it. But it is the only way I know to explain the men who made up Blue's Bastards and the extraordinary record they compiled in that bloody and unpopular war.

SETTLING IN

THE FIRST WEEK or two I just sat around and listened to war stories. What I heard was talk laced with a vocabulary that I didn't understand. "Sweeps," "sparrow hawking," "firefight" were not terms I'd heard in boot camp. Now I was hearing them every other word; and I didn't want to ask what they meant; so I sat, listened, and eventually figured them all out.

The most important were the words or phrases that described types of actions:

SWEEPING

A "sweep" consisted of reconnoitering the countryside on foot with the intention of seeking out the enemy and destroying him. In its most basic elements a sweep was simply a hunting party assigned to a particular area. You went out in groups, fully armed, your eyes peeled for movement or other signs of the prey; and when you flushed a covey of North Vietnamese, you shot them or else blew them away with heavier weaponry. You made company sweeps, platoon sweeps, and even squad sweeps; and if you didn't think about it too much, you could imag-

ine that you were back in the Oklahoma woods
on a cool fall day, out to bag your limit.

But of course there were at least two big differences between hunting in Vietnam and hunting in the United States. First, in Vietnam you
were hunting human beings rather than quail
and deer. For this reason, you didn't see the prey
as often and so your thoughts weren't as clear or
as satisfying. And it was usually impossible to
verify a kill. Typically you were directing your
fire toward a burst of flame or a bunker. No target soared through the air or dashed out into a
clearing, paused, and looked around while you
took aim and squeezed off a round. So there
were few clean kills and, of course, no trophies
to mount on the wall.

More importantly, however, deer, quail, and
other game in the United States don't threaten
your life. I suppose sitting in a blind on an Afri-
can safari, waiting for a rhino, or following a
wounded lion into high grass would involve
some of the elements of risk found in our kind
of hunting—but not enough to count. We were,
after all, the hunted as well as the hunters. Any
moment during a sweep could have been our
last. We could have blundered onto a well-en-
trenched enemy position and been mowed down
before we had a chance to take cover. We could
have been ambushed even in the most open
country. And if that weren't worry enough, we
were constantly harassed by sniper fire. You
never knew when a round would suddenly bury
itself deep in your chest, a shot you never heard,
fired by someone you never saw. And that was
one reason why Blue ordered us to keep our

steel helmets on at all times, with the chin straps buckled.

Sweeps were our main activity during those months. Sometimes we would be out for forty and fifty days, nosing around in the bush, probing various hillsides, hunting for enemy fighting units that were in turn hunting for us.

SPARROW HAWKING

Sparrow hawking was a little less strenuous than sweeping, but maybe more dangerous. When you sparrow hawked, you sat on a "duster" and hunted the enemy, the way some people sit on the fender of a jeep and hunt rabbits. A duster was a light, armored vehicle with twin 40-mm cannons. We used to ride out on these tanks to relieve other outfits that had been hit hard, and once to help the Army Corps of Engineers, who were trying to build a road between outposts. Needless to say, the enemy snipers had a field day with the road workers, so we were sent out to make their sport a little riskier.

When we sparrow hawked we were what the Marines called an Instantaneous Reactionary Force. We would load onto the dusters, about twelve men per tank, and move into the target area, then wait for the enemy to attack the apparently crippled or defenseless unit. As soon as they made their move we would roar down on them, set up, and with the support of the tanks give them everything we had in the way of firepower. Usually they would turn tail and run, though sometimes they were tempted by the tanks.

There were two reasons why sparrow hawk-

ing was maybe a little more dangerous than
sweeping. First, there was the danger of falling
off the tank. Tanks, after all, are not luxury vehi-
cles. They are not built with anybody's comfort
in mind, and when you hit a bump you don't
have shock absorbers to save wear and tear on
your spine. As a matter of fact, when you suddenly swoop down into a hollow or start up a
hill, a tank is harder to hang on to than an electric bull. You could break an arm or leg falling
off a tank as quickly as you could while riding in
a rodeo. Lieutenant North himself had broken
his ribs and punctured a lung under such circumstances. (In his case, however, he'd just begun to fight. He dragged himself to his feet,
grabbed an M-79 grenade launcher, and
knocked out an enemy machine gun nest, for
which he was awarded the Bronze Star.)

But the main reason why sparrow hawking
was dangerous had to do with the attitude of the
North Vietnamese troops: They loved to blow up
tanks, and they were very good at it. Tanks were
easy to spot and easier to hear. They usually
traveled in more open terrain. And when you
knocked out a tank, you scored major points,
since you killed at least two people and destroyed an important piece of weaponry. So the
enemy would concentrate on a tank when he
had the opportunity.

DIGGING IN

Sometimes we would be asked to hold a position for a while, knowing the enemy would
have to attack us and in so doing expose himself.
Some of the toughest fighting we experienced

was on top of Mutter's Ridge when we dug in and then waited for the inevitable bombardment at Happy Hour. In fact, it was during such attacks that we were most vulnerable, since we had very little room in which to maneuver. When you're moving through the bush and are attacked by snipers or by an enemy patrol, you can at least take evasive action or launch a counterattack. But when you're dug in on a hillside, stuck in your foxhole, all you can do is listen to the sound of the enemy guns and then hear and feel the explosions all around you.

Most of the time the enemy fire was off-target, but one day—when they got our coordinates—they were dropping mortar shells into foxholes like basketballs through hoops. It was the most helpless feeling in the world to hunch down inside the hole and wonder if the next one was going to land on your head.

You could hear the shells being dropped into the mortar tube—*thunk, thunk, thunk*. When you heard that sound, suddenly you stopped what you were doing and saying and listened. You knew that one second after you heard the fifth *thunk*, the first round would hit somewhere in your general vicinity—and maybe right in your lap. So you slid deeper into your foxhole and began to pray. It was probably the toughest part of fighting in Vietnam—at least for me.

STANDING LINES

When we returned to C-2 after sweeps or sparrow hawking, we still had to "stand lines," or "pull guard duty." Only over there it was no mere exercise, the way it was in boot camp. We all knew there was a real danger the enemy would be out there. As a matter of fact, if you stood lines long enough you were sure to draw sniper fire at some point. Then the whole company would be blasting away, and for the next ten or fifteen minutes it would sound like World War III.

When we stood lines we lived in a crescent of fighting holes in between the camp and the enemy. In front of us was a snarl of concertina wire and beyond that a field of pre-set trip flares and pre-set Claymore mines. The Claymores gave us a real sense of security, because they were among the deadliest and messiest weapons we had. They were filled with an explosive and a bunch of steel bearings the size of marbles. They were curved, and we would plant the mines so that the concave sides were facing our way and the convex sides were aimed in the direction of enemy lines. Then we would wire them up to a detonator box (the "hell box") powered by a half-volt battery. The hell box was manned by Bob Mullins; and if anyone attacked us, Mullins was to push the plunger and send a thousand steel bearings whizzing into the night. We figured that any North Vietnamese out there would end up with two or three more eyes in his face than he started out with.

STAND-DOWN TIME

Party time. Sack time. Lying around time. There wasn't much of this in the Marine Corps, not while I was in service. Sometimes, after we'd been sweeping for weeks and weeks, we'd get to fall back to Quang Tri or Razorback and pull a little sack time, play some cards, and drink a few cold beers at night. But we seldom had more than a day or two to lie around, fewer days off than an office worker had. Our "office" was Leatherneck Square or Mutter's Ridge, and we kept strict hours seven days a week, including most Federal holidays.

FIREFIGHT

A battle. A heavy encounter with the enemy. Any engagement larger than running into sniper fire. Most of the firefights we experienced eventually involved artillery fire and mortars. Sometimes the enemy used rocket-propelled grenades (RPGs) as well, but only when we were fighting almost hand to hand. The North Vietnamese rockets, like the old bazookas, were fired at close range by infantrymen.

A firefight involving all of these weapons is easier to describe than to define. You're crouched in a foxhole staring into the twilight, or stretched out on the side of the ridge, sound asleep, when suddenly in the distance you hear the first *thunk* of an enemy mortar or the roar of artillery, and within seconds explosions are going off on all sides of you. You're in the middle of flashing lights, ear-splitting booms, and flying metal. It's an understatement to say it's like a particularly brilliant 4th of July celebration. It's more like standing inside a fireworks factory when somebody forgets and strikes a match. You aren't just watching from a safe distance. You're at the center of it, only the explosions are ten times louder than any firecracker or toy rocket, and the flashes are 100 times brighter. And though you pray for it to stop, you're even more afraid that any second the whole scene will suddenly go blank, and you won't hear noises or see lights because you'll be dead.

At that point all you can do is hope that somebody calls in artillery and air strikes before a mortar or artillery shell drops into your foxhole and turns you into red jelly. I've seen corpsmen carrying bags filled with what was left of direct hits; and while it's the quickest way to go, it's also the messiest. You can't help thinking about such things when you're in a foxhole during a firefight, unable to strike back effectively or even to move.

I had time to absorb all this military lore, because after a couple of days we moved from Vandergriff Combat Base up to C-2, where we were ordered to stand by and help the first Marine outfit that got into trouble and needed reinforcements. While we were there we got our shots, had haircuts, and stocked up with C-rations, ammunition, and other personal supplies. We stayed for about a month, and had little to do except stand lines and drink beer. I'll say this, beer was cheap—only 15 cents a can—but you could only have two cans a day so it was hardly worth it. That's why Ernie Tuten and I would store ours up for three or four days and have a real party out in the fighting holes. Even then we didn't get drunk, but at least we knew we'd been drinking beer.

After a few days at C-2 we got orders to move out. The 9th Marines were in trouble, the Walking Dead. They'd gotten into a firefight and suffered heavy casualties. Now they were pinned down and in danger of being overrun. I remembered the look on the faces of the guys who'd been sent there, and I wondered how many of them were already dead. Now we would be fighting side by side with them.

We would be sparrow hawking, a first time for me. After packing our gear, the whole squad piled onto a duster; and as I expected, it was a lot easier than trekking through the bush. The duster moved at about 20 miles per hour, which wasn't really fast until you considered that you weren't driving down the interstate but over some of the roughest terrain a tank ever covered at that speed. We were crossing Leatherneck Square, and I don't think we missed a single bomb crater. Half the time we were flying through the air and half the time we were slapping against the steel of the tank.

Somewhere along the way the 9th Marines radioed to tell us that things were under control, that they'd beaten back the enemy and were preparing to move on. No need for reinforcements. That was good news for the 9th Marines, though they'd still sustained heavy casualties. I was glad we hadn't tied in with them. They were a hard-luck outfit.

On the way back I was a little more relaxed, and a little less careful. Sitting near the edge of the tank I was too busy talking to see the huge dip in the landscape that lay just ahead, and suddenly the tank dived out from under me and for an instant I was suspended in air. Then I slapped back down onto the tank's hard top, rolled toward the edge, and grabbed wildly at anything I could get my hands on. What I grabbed turned out to be Sal, the grinning Indonesian; and we both rolled off the tank and fell into bushes and stumps. I outweighed Sal by about 60 pounds; and as fate would have it, I landed on top of him. He came up still grinning, obviously unhurt. But when I got to my feet I thought I might have broken my hand.

We climbed back on the tank; and when we got back to C-2, I checked with the corpsman. Sure enough, the bone was cracked. So I was out of action for several weeks and assigned to do mess duty during the daytime, though I still stood lines at night. Not the best duty, but it turned out that one of the new mess sergeants was a guy I'd known from Oklahoma City. So we talked a lot about people and places we both knew, drank some cold beer, and time passed pretty quickly.

One night, however, I got my first taste of sniper fire. I was propped up in my foxhole, staring up at the stars, when suddenly about eight rounds came whistling in from the darkness and kicked up dirt around me. Almost before I could get my weapon up to my shoulder, the trip flares went off and it looked like the whole countryside was in flames. I peered out across the field as the flares flickered and faded, but no one was there, so I relaxed a little. Then from behind me I heard the roar of semi-automatics and machine guns. It sounded like everybody in camp was blasting away into the empty night, and I instinctively ducked down so I wouldn't get the back of my head torn off. Then the firing stopped as suddenly as it had begun.

I had the feeling that the North Vietnamese would fire a few shots at us, then lie back and laugh while we pumped several hundred rounds into an empty field. But you never knew when they would be coming; and sometimes they did, even at C-2, though never in large numbers, and they always fell back quickly in the face of superior firepower.

One day, when I was hanging around the mess hall, my Oklahoma City buddy gave me the best present I could have gotten, short of an early discharge—a whole case of beer.

"The day after tomorrow's the 4th of July," he said. "You can take this back and have a real celebration."

"I can if there's some way I can smuggle it out to the perimeter," I told him, and I scouted around for an hour before I came up with the right means. I found an empty mortar shell box, took the case of beer, stashed it inside, and packed the space between the two boxes with sand. But why would I be bringing mortars up to the perimeter? I thought about it for a while and finally came up with a story. I would tell the guys that these were trip flares to be used for a 4th of July celebration, that we weren't to touch them until the day after tomorrow. When it got dark, I'd take the box and bury it somewhere until the 4th. Then we'd sure-enough have a party.

I waited until it was dusk before I attempted to move my cargo. When I got back to the foxhole Manilla asked me what I had, and I told him my story. He seemed only mildly interested, and I set the box behind the bunker and tried not to think about it. The guy I was mainly worried about was Redmon, who was in a foxhole somewhere down the line. He had always said he could smell beer, even when it hadn't been opened; and while I didn't necessarily believe him, I didn't want to take any chances. I didn't see him around, so I breathed a little easier.

After dark, I got the beer, still in its disguise, and took it back to a "hooch" tent where we slept in the daytime, and buried the box in the sand. For some reason the idea of Redmon's supersensory powers bothered me, so I took some extra time digging, and planted the box three feet deep underground. If it had been a week-old corpse Redmon couldn't have smelled it.

Then I went back to the row of fighting holes and began to shoot the bull with Al Manilla and Leroy Terry.

"Where's Redmon?" I asked casually. "I haven't seen him lately."

"He's around," said Leroy, and I let the matter drop.

About a half hour later Redmon came strolling up and I waved at him, as casually as I knew how.

"Where is it?" he said.

"Where's what?" I said, still confident.

"Where's the case of beer you buried around here?"

I couldn't believe my ears; and though somehow I knew I was beaten, I tried to bluff it out.

"Where could I possibly get a case of beer?"

"I don't know where you got it," he said, "but I know it's here somewhere."

"Then find it," I said.

Redmon turned, seemed to sniff the wind, and then walked straight over and stopped at the spot where I'd buried the box.

"I'd say it was right here," he said.

I couldn't believe it. It had been pitch dark when I'd buried the box. No one could have seen me. No one. And if they had, they wouldn't have known it was beer.

"I was saving it for the 4th," I said.

"To hell with the 4th," said Redmon. "Let's drink it now."

So we did, and while I asked him a number of times how he knew it was there, he would just shrug his shoulders and say, "I smelled it."

On the 4th it was announced that we would eat a hot meal flown in for the occasion, compliments of the U.S. government. So at the time specified we lined up, with mess gear if we had it, paper plates if we didn't; but the choppers were late. Finally, when they did arrive, it took them about an hour to set up the chow line, and when we were actually served the meal, it was cold. But it didn't matter. We were glad to get it anyway, and we never expected it to be hot in the first place.

Later that afternoon we were told we could draw new ammunition and then fire off all the old rounds in honor of the occasion. So there we were, a bunch of American teenagers, shooting off our rifles just to hear the noise, when almost any day of the week we could expect to fire them at the enemy in self-defense. It was an odd thing to do, but we got a big kick out of it. Then they gave us a couple of beers or a couple of ounces of whisky, whichever we preferred; and we figured we'd been treated to a great 4th of July party.

FIREFIGHT

ON A MORNING in the middle of July—about five weeks after I had broken my hand—I was in the supply room of the camp mess hall, breaking open crates of C-rations, when the clerk who worked at the infirmary stuck his head into the room and told me the doctor wanted to see me immediately. I was a little puzzled, but I walked over to the next Quonset hut, to find the doctor waiting for me, a frown on his face. He motioned for me to follow him into his cubicle; and with a grave look he reached into a drawer and pulled out a pair of shears as big as hedge clippers.

"Herrod," he said, "I've got pretty bad news for you."

I eyed the shears nervously and asked him what was wrong.

"I'm going to cut off your cast. Then you'll have to report back to active duty and get your ass shot at again."

Actually, I was glad to be rid of the hot cast and relieved that the doctor didn't find some kind of terminal skin disease when he finally peeled it off. I was even glad to get back to active duty—though I had enjoyed hanging around the mess hall, shooting the breeze with the mess sergeant from Oklahoma—because I was getting bored, and one thing was certain—when you were in combat, life was never boring. As I walked the dusty mile across the camp, flexing my brand new hand, it occurred to me that I was beginning to like combat.

And a good thing I was. When I got to Kilo Company and stepped into my squad tent, everybody was at his own bunk, getting his backpack ready. Manilla looked up and grinned at me.

"Great timing, Herrod," he said. "We're moving out in about 30 minutes. Get your gear packed."

"Where are we going?" I asked.

"First Sergeant says Mutter's Ridge," said Frenchy, "and he's probably right."

"Just the platoon?" I asked.

"All of Kilo Company," said Manilla.

About ten minutes later Lieutenant North came through the door, looked around, and spotted me.

He walked over, smiling.

"Good to have you back," he said, shaking hands with a firm grip. "How's the hand?"

The question was a mere formality. He was finding out how my hand was at that very moment, putting as much pressure on it as he could, forcing me to squeeze back.

"It's okay," I said. "I can pull a trigger."

"That's not the only thing that matters," he said, "but it's the most important thing. Let me know if you have any problems."

Then he wheeled and was gone. A few minutes later he inspected our gear just before we boarded the helicopter to fly to the edge of the desert. As always, he checked us one at a time, like a scoutmaster inspecting his troop—going over the usual things: rifles, grenade pins, helmet straps. Same old ritual, but all of us felt a little more secure as we climbed on the plane.

None of us liked the idea of Mutter's Ridge, if only because it meant marching north across the desert waste of Leatherneck Square—about 35 miles of hot sand, bomb craters, charred stumps, and a few twisted stalks of elephant grass—and then scaling the steep cliffside. We had already been there four times since I had joined the platoon. I suppose it was important because it was high ground on the DMZ and gave us a lookout post from which to monitor enemy troops crossing the border; but the problem was, we never held it long enough to make any difference. It would take us three or four days to get there and about three hours for the North Vietnamese to drive us down from the ridge and send us humping back across Leatherneck Square. As we were swept into the air, that's what most of us were thinking about.

"Hey, Lieutenant," Manilla yelled over the roar of the helicopter engines, "I heard some tanks will be escorting us. That right?"

"That's what I hear, too," Lieutenant North yelled back.

"Then how about us hitching a ride on the tanks when we get to Leatherneck Square?"

North shook his head.

"Can't do it. You'd all be sitting ducks for snipers. Besides, Herrod would fall off and break his hand again."

I laughed with the rest of them, but in fact I burned with shame at the memory of what I'd done the last time I rode a tank. And North's kidding reminded me to be more careful this time, in whatever I was doing.

"Besides, things will be a little different this time," said Lieutenant North. "We've located a number of trails the enemy has been using lately, mostly at night. So we'll be moving during the daytime and setting up night ambushes."

The helicopter set us down about five miles into Leatherneck Square, and we hauled our backpacks onto our shoulders and started humping toward the distant foothills, rifles in hand, waiting for the first sign of North Vietnamese troops. Ordinarily they hid out all day, but we weren't taking any chances.

Still, I felt a lot safer when the tanks came roaring up from behind to join us. There were twelve of them, spaced evenly among the platoons of Kilo Company, which had a fighting strength of about 150 men. With Captain Goodwin in command of the company, and Blue in command of our platoon, we were spread out to form a line about 200 yards wide; and while a sniper could still get in a shot or two and then run, it was highly unlikely that we would suddenly have to face a frontal attack by an enemy infantry unit. Not with the tanks riding shotgun.

The first day in the field Blue's Bastards drew a day patrol, followed by a night ambush. On a patrol, the 50 of us would move out ahead in small groups, probing the hills and hollows, trying to locate enemy camps or spot enemy movement. On a night ambush we would position ourselves on a hill overlooking a known trail and then hope the North Vietnamese would come down it, though usually we sat there, staring into the darkness, until the sun came up.

That night we set up the ambush, while back at the command post Captain Goodwin ordered the tanks to form a circle around the company of about a hundred yards in diameter, and the other two platoons stood perimeter watch all night, scanning the flat, dead land for signs of movement.

The next day, instead of marching on, the company took up a position on the top of a small hill. Since we had been on patrol the previous day and up all night as well, Blue's Bastards stayed back in the perimeter and slept while the 1st Platoon went on patrol, and set up another night ambush. Back inside the perimeter it was at least 120 degrees, so hot that during the day most of us could only catch a few minutes of sleep, even under the shade of small hooch tents.

At about 1100 hours a couple of helicopters landed with resupplies, and a lance corporal we'd never seen before came over and began talking to Lieutenant North. Then the two of them walked to where Romeo and Leroy Terry were using their entrenching tools to dig a two-man foxhole. So Al and I, who were digging our own foxhole, stopped and joined them. I knew what was happening immediately. Romeo was a short-timer and this would be his replacement. Sure enough, when we got there Romeo was already getting his gear together.

So he'd made it through. I was glad for him, but sorry at the same time, because he had been a good friend. For an instant I thought of how it would be if I were on my way back to Oklahoma. But I quickly put the idea out of my head. No use to think about home for another year.

Blue introduced us to the new guy, but I didn't catch his name. Then we shook hands with Romeo, while he smiled and avoided our eyes, the way he always did. He loaded his gear on board, then climbed in himself and gave one final wave. It wasn't until I watched the helicopter swing up into the bright sky that I thought about what Romeo's departure might mean to the gun team. But Blue was already on top of the situation. He talked to the new guy, who, it turned out, wasn't a new guy at all but a transfer from another unit, with plenty of combat experience on a machine gun team.

"Okay," said Blue, "here's the way it goes. He's got more time in-country than Herrod, but less than Manilla; so Manilla moves to team leader and the corporal here takes over as gunner. Herrod, you'll still be A-gunner and ammo humper. Congratulations."

Lieutenant North grinned, and that was it. He'd played it by the book, and I had no complaints. So the new guy came back to the foxhole with me, and Manilla went over to join Leroy Terry. Then we finished our foxholes, though we didn't dig them too deep since we knew we'd be moving out again at daybreak.

I talked some with the new guy, but he was as beat as I was; so we tried to catch some sack time. After dark we all moved out in front of the perimeter and set up our trip flares and Claymore mines. As usual, I found myself hoping the enemy would try to move in across the field, because I'd always wanted to see the trap sprung, with blazing lights and a thousand steel ball bearings flying through the air. (One night a few months later, my wish would come true, though not exactly the way I'd hoped.)

After we came back, I was hungry so I pinched off a chunk of C-4 explosive plastic, lit it, and cooked my can of C-rations. By this time I'd developed a little ritual that I repeated throughout my tour in Vietnam. I called it my "Last Supper," and I only performed it when I was out on patrol or knew I was going to be sent into a combat zone the next day. It consisted of nothing more than taking out a can of my favorite C-ration dinner, which was chicken and rice, heating it up, and slowly savoring it. Originally I did this because, like the proverbial condemned man, I wanted to eat a hearty meal before I died. Later, however, after I had survived a number of close calls, it became a kind of good luck charm to ward off bullets, the sort of thing a baseball manager does when he wears the same underwear every day because his team is on a winning streak.

So that evening, with Romeo winging his way back to the States and with an unknown quantity joining the team, I had been particularly careful to cook up a Last Supper—as always, chicken and rice.

Fortunately, I stood watch from eight to midnight, which meant I wouldn't have to wake up in the middle of the night and then try to get back to sleep again. There was a tank stationed immediately to our left, and I saw something moving out just beyond where the tank was. It was Frenchy, on his way to relieve the guy at the listening post, out in a shallow foxhole about fifty meters beyond the perimeter.

He saw me and came over.

"Damn, it's a good night for sleeping," he said. "After this watch, I'm going back and sacking out."

"It's cold," I said. "It's probably below 100 degrees."

"Yeah," said Frenchy. "I'm putting on my extra socks."

He waved and was gone.

The watch passed slowly, and I spent most of my time watching the sky just over the rim of the horizon, looking for shooting stars; but it was a bad night for them. Finally twelve o'clock came, and after talking with the new guy some more, I called it a day. I was hoping to get some real sleep, mostly because it actually had begun to turn cool. As a matter of fact, by the time I stretched out on the side of the hill, it was downright cold for July, probably about 90 degrees; so I decided to take off my flak jacket, use it as a blanket, and take full advantage of the air conditioning. Tomorrow I knew it would be back up to 120 degrees again. Al Manilla did the same thing, and the new guy and Leroy Terry curled up in the two-man foxholes.

I was right. The night air seemed chilly, and it had been easy to go to sleep, even though I was lying on a slanted hillside. I had never been so comfortable. Suddenly, at about 0300 hours, a rocket exploded within a few yards of where I was stretched out, and I awoke to find myself flying through the air, then tumbling down the hillside.

My first impulse was sheer terror, but as I skidded through the brush on my butt, I thought I knew what had happened. Then I was angry.

"Stupid tank," I shouted, convinced one of them had fired off a round by accident.

"It's not the tanks," Leroy Terry shouted from somewhere. "It's the gooks."

By the time I came to my senses, explosions were shaking the hill on every side, and the world was a blaze of orange and white lights. In addition, tracer bullets were whining in and ricocheting off the tanks. It sounded like a shooting gallery.

At that instant I had the eerie feeling that I was already dead, that my mind hadn't quite caught up with the fact. I ran toward the sound of Terry's voice, and out of the corner of my eye I saw Manilla. He'd been knocked down the hill by the concussion too, and he was scrambling for the same foxhole I was. We both made it at the same time and dived, forgetting that Leroy Terry, the biggest man in the platoon, was already in there. I landed on Leroy's butt, and Manilla landed on his head. For all we knew, we'd driven him a foot into the sand, but we continued to grind into him, trying to get down as low as we could, while explosions erupted and metal fragments kept banging off the sides of the tanks.

Neither Al nor I had a helmet on, and we could hear bullets sailing between our heads. We shouted at Leroy to sit up so we could get off his back. Then all three of us could burrow down in the foxhole. But when he tried to lift his head, he hoisted Manilla up into the line of fire; and when he raised his butt, he did the same thing to me. So we were trapped. If bullets hadn't been whistling all around us, it would have been funny. But instead of laughing, we screamed at each other in wild panic.

We might have just crouched there and hoped to hell nothing skimmed the ground low enough to hit us, but we knew we couldn't do that and live. This was no artillery or mortar attack. What had hit the tank next to us was a rocket round, and the bullets whizzing just over our heads were fired by small arms. We were not being bombarded by mortars stationed five miles away. Some force was close enough to fire at us with rifles. We were being attacked by ground troops! The next time I popped my head up I saw them: dark figures scrambling up the hillside, then flashes of light as the barrels of their rifles blazed.

I was suddenly afraid, realizing that in a matter of moments I might be in hand-to-hand combat. I listened, but to our left no one was firing. The tank was out of action. That meant that our segment of the perimeter was unprotected. They had created a hole in our defenses and now were trying to break through. The perimeter needed our firepower. Otherwise our position would be overrun, and in a couple of minutes we'd have little men standing over us, firing down into our faces.

Through the rocket blasts and the whining of bullets Manilla noticed something—or rather the absence of something. The new guy wasn't firing the machine gun. One more reason why our segment of the perimeter was in danger.

"The gun," Manilla yelled above the roar. "Go over there and see what's wrong."

I looked at him in disbelief.

"I ain't about to get out of this hole," I shouted back.

"Something's wrong," he yelled. "Go over and see."

"Like hell. You're the team leader," I told him. "It's your gun. You go."

When the next explosion lit the hillside, I saw that Manilla had been hit in the arms, neck, and left side of his jaw. He was patched with blood and for an instant I was worried he was about to keel over on me. Then I realized he wasn't in any danger. He'd been hit by a spray of small shrapnel fragments—something slightly worse than being wounded by a B-B gun. But now he had a good excuse for not risking his butt on that run to the next foxhole.

"You lucky bastard," I shouted; and cursing all the way, I scrambled out and zigzagged over to the other foxhole, aware with every step that I didn't have on my flak jacket or my steel helmet. On the way I looked down at my arm and saw I'd been torn up by shrapnel too. Only when I saw the blood did my arm start to sting in several places. I remember thinking it was just my luck to see Manilla's wounds before I saw my own.

Crouching as low as I could, I made it to the foxhole where I should have been sleeping and saw the new guy hunched over the gun.

"Why don't you fire it?" I shouted, trying to see how best to get down in there with him. Meanwhile the sky was lit up every couple of seconds by blinding flashes, and the hillside was continually rocking from the explosions.

"I'm blind," he screamed. "I'm blind! I can't see."

I looked down and saw that his face was a splash of blood. I couldn't tell whether his features had been blown away or he'd been hit in the forehead by shrapnel. Probably the latter. I felt sorry for him, but at the same time I was annoyed that he was screaming so loud. He was just one more problem I had to deal with, and probably the least important. If he would just shut up!

I jumped down into the foxhole, pushed him out of the way, put on his helmet, and then looked out for the first time. The enemy was already halfway up the hill, maybe 75 yards away. I could see their silhouettes and then the flash of their rifle muzzles, but I couldn't tell if any of them were being hit. For a moment I was certain we were about to be overrun, and I was terrified. I thought about turning tail and running, but there was no place to hide. Then off to my left I saw a tank laying down a field of fire with tracers, so I grabbed the machine gun, watched, and where he stopped I started—firing in bursts of eight rounds. We were doing it by the book, laying down intersecting fields of fire. When he stopped I'd start, and when I stopped he'd start.

Then I wondered what had happened to the tanks on either side. I glanced to the one on my left, about 15 feet away. It was a smoking shell. The blast that had knocked me down the hill had scored a direct hit. The one on my right was out too. I figured the guys inside were dead or unconscious, because no one was firing the guns. So for this part of the perimeter, I was it.

Suddenly a voice behind me shouted, "Keep firing, Herrod. Keep firing."

It was Blue. He was standing about ten feet

behind me, directing the platoon's fire, shouting into the telephone, in full view of the enemy. If you were charging a hill, you'd never want a better target. But he didn't appear to be bothered by the fact that bullets were bouncing off the tank next to him like heavy hail. I had watched him under fire before, but never at such close range. He was the kind of battlefield commander you saw in old movies—calm, oblivious to danger, concerned only with the problem at hand, which was saving his platoon from being overrun and blown to bits. And he went about his task with such cool concentration you'd think he was standing in a telephone booth on Main Street. I didn't have much time to think about it; but when I did, I was envious. I would have given anything for that much courage.

Something else also occurred to me. Being so near someone manning a machine gun didn't help his chances a bit, since the silhouettes were beginning to concentrate their firepower on me. In fact, by all odds both of us should have been dead already. I thought to myself, "Every second I live now, I'll be beating the seven-second survival average for a machine gunner in combat."

To my far left I saw that some of the enemy were no more than twenty feet from the perimeter, and the tank whose field of fire I had been intersecting lowered its sights, fired, and then leaped forward. The running silhouettes hesitated, then turned. But it was too late for two of them. The tank ran them down, then roared into reverse, and took its place back in line.

I continued to fire bursts out in front of me, and I could see black silhouettes fall to the ground, though I couldn't be sure whether or not they'd been hit. One thing was certain: they were still coming, and I could see the flashes of their gun muzzles maybe fifty yards away.

I heard a roar over to my left and saw a huge explosion just down the hill, with silhouettes flying in every direction. Leroy Terry had gotten off a rocket. And he had three more. Meanwhile, Manilla, who still had the use of his right side, was firing his M-16, which helped draw a little fire away from me. There were so many bullets whining around me by then that I wasn't sure I'd survive to get off another burst. But North was still standing tall behind me, shouting out orders, so I figured I had no real complaints. I popped up and began firing again, and some more silhouettes hit the ground.

"My God," screamed the new guy. "I'm blind!"

Then about forty yards in front of me, I saw a huge orange flame and a roar erupted just to my rear. The concussion almost finished my eardrums, and I looked back just in time to see Blue crumple and pitch forward, the back of his legs torn up by shrapnel. A rocket. It had hit the tank and then exploded. The blast had knocked the lieutenant unconscious, and he lay about four feet away, bullets whining all around.

I could see that he was moving a little, so I crawled halfway out of the hole, grabbed him by the arm, and hauled him back toward me, my back feeling completely naked. Then, when he was next to the foxhole, I climbed all the way out, propped up on one elbow, and shielding him with my body, I began firing bursts at the rapidly closing enemy. By then Blue was already regaining consciousness, and I put down the machine gun to help him climb into the foxhole, though there wasn't enough room for the three of us. For an instant his glazed eyes met mine, while Terry fired off another rocket round. Then there was the light of recognition.

"Keep firing!" he barked at me, and though I wasn't sure he knew what he was saying, I let go of him, wheeled, and grabbed up the machine gun again. When he gave an order, you instinctively obeyed.

It was a good thing I did! There were two of them about twenty-five feet away, just off to the left. I wheeled, gave them a couple of quick bursts, and they went down. We were about to be infiltrated, and when that happened they'd be firing into my back as well as into my face.

"Oh, my God!" screamed the new guy.

I glanced back at Blue, and he was up on one knee, yelling into the phone again, so I turned and continued firing at the scrambling shapes that flashed fire and then fell to the ground. It was eerie. Suddenly a chill gripped my heart. The same shapes were going down and rising again. They weren't being hit when they fell. They were just protecting themselves between moves. They continued to lunge forward, two or three steps at a time, but always closer.

I tried to guess how many rounds I had left. We'd begun with approximately 2,000, and I'd already fired off a bunch. Then I realized that it really didn't matter. I'd fire till I ran out. Then use my M-14. No use to conserve rounds when they were practically in our faces.

The new guy screamed with pain again, and I remembered something. I'd left my flak jacket out on the ground, but he was wearing a web belt full of hand grenades. I reached over and practically tore it off him. When I looked up again, two silhouettes were twenty-five feet in front of me, so instead of throwing the grenade I just pulled the pin, stuck my arm up, and rolled the thing down the hill. The earth shook, and when I peered out, the silhouettes had turned to dark lumps on the ground.

Thank God, I thought. They weren't invulnerable. They could be killed, even if it took grenades to do it. It was the first inkling I had that we might be able to drive them back, and the thought made me feel a little calmer.

At this stage we were practically an infantry unit, since all but three or four of the tanks had been knocked out. Neither the one to my right nor the one to my left was firing anything; and I still heard no signs of life, so I figured the guys inside were fried. But down the way, one was still operational, and maybe a couple more were firing behind me.

I pulled the pin on another grenade and without looking out, rolled it down the hill. As soon as the earth shook, I popped up and started firing again. One thing was certain—the grenades were clearing the area in the immediate vicinity, and I wished I'd had thirty or forty more.

Things were desperate for another ten minutes. Every time I looked up they'd be coming again, and it would take a grenade to clear them out. I thought there must have been a thousand of them out there, because no matter how many we blew away, they kept coming.

Then the moment arrived when I realized

they weren't coming up as fast and their numbers weren't quite as great. I felt a sudden surge of adrenaline, and at the same time my muscles began to relax a little. It was exhilarating. We were beating the enemy. At some point we'd reached an equilibrium, and for a long while after that, both sides maintained their positions and kept up the firing. I'd see movement and I'd get off a few bursts, then duck while a bullet or two whistled over my head. They weren't using rockets anymore, which meant they'd probably run out. If we could just hold on until dawn, we could call in an air strike and they'd be history. But they understood that hard truth as well as we did. I knew by daylight they'd be gone.

After about three hours of frequent exchanges, the black sky turned to silver-gray, and by the time it was red and blue, they'd slipped away, all except the ones sprawled in awkward and unlikely positions in front of us. As daylight flooded the landscape they turned from gray hulks to definable shapes, maybe twenty-five of them just in front of me, all the way down the hillside, glowing in the sunlight as if they were on fire; and already the flies were swarming around them, like tiny golden specks of sun.

"You okay?"

I turned and saw North standing just behind me. I had forgotten about him for the last couple of hours, but I was glad to see he'd made it.

"I'm fine," I said. "How about you?"

He nodded.

"Can't complain," he said. "Thanks for the help."

Then the new guy groaned, and we both remembered. North helped him scramble out of the foxhole, and started to lead him away.

"Don't leave," he called back. "It'll be 100 percent watch until we get reinforcements."

I watched him as he walked away, the back of his legs gouged and still bleeding; and I remembered myself, crouching in the foxhole, sometimes even holding the machine gun over my head to fire off bursts, rather than stick my face above ground. I was a pretty sorry excuse for a Marine compared to Blue, who had exposed himself the whole time without diving for cover once.

I remember thinking: What kind of man is he to be so absolutely unafraid? Is he so numb inside that he has no feelings at all? Or is he just perfectly disciplined every second of his life? Knowing the depth of his concern for his men, I figured it had to be the latter, but that still made him a different kind of human being from the rest of us.

On balance, however, I was content with the fact that I had plugged up the hole in my part of the dike and that I was able to help Blue when he needed it. All I had to do now was manage to stay awake for the next few hours.

I sat there and scanned the landscape, hoping to see the enemy in the light of day, but I knew better. After about ten minutes I heard a faint buzz and then the drone of engines in the sky. It was the Hueys, and they came on fast, but we all knew they were much too late. What was left of that enemy battalion or regiment or army was off hiding somewhere, licking its wounds and counting its dead, already planning a new attack.

A few minutes later I heard the medevac choppers, and I knew they'd be treating the wounded, then flying them out—including the new guy. It looked as if he wouldn't be gunner after all. I wondered what his name was.

Then I realized that the helicopters would also be bringing body bags to haul out the dead —our dead. There would be a lot of them this day, and for the first time I wondered about Manilla and Terry in the next foxhole, but I was too beat to drag myself over there or even to call.

I did crawl out of the foxhole, and sit on the edge, wondering if I'd be able to keep my balance or if I'd topple back in like a rag doll. After about five minutes Jim Honey came across the perimeter and went over to the other foxhole. Terry's head appeared and Honey said something to him.

I signaled Honey and he came over to join me.

"Al's okay," he said. "They're getting ready to fly him out right now."

I felt a great sense of relief. I hadn't realized it, but in the back of my mind I had been worrying about him. Manilla was a cocky little bastard who cracked too many bad jokes; but he was an important part of my life, particularly since Romeo was gone.

"What about the new guy, the one who was here with me?"

"With the eyes?"

I nodded, too tired to waste words.

"He's okay, too. Corpsman said his eyes weren't really damaged. Just full of blood."

"That's good," I said, meaning it, sorry I had been so annoyed at the poor guy.

I looked up at him.

"All of our others guys make it?"

He shook his head.

"Frenchy," he said.

"Frenchy?"

He nodded.

"They dropped a rocket right in on top of him. He probably never even heard it coming."

I shook my head in disbelief. I'd talked to him at the change of guard. I tried to concentrate, to gauge the shock, to remember what he looked like; but for some reason his face eluded me. I kept seeing Romeo. At that moment I couldn't even feel sorrow, only an ache spreading through my entire body. I remember thinking I would have to write Kay.

"But that was all in our platoon," Honey said, trying to be upbeat. "A bunch more bought it, a whole bunch. But not any more of the Bastards. Just Frenchy."

As I listened to him, I was staring down into the foxhole at the new guy's web belt, the one I'd jerked off him in the heat of the firefight. It was on fire, and I watched as the cloth weave in the belt turned slowly black while the flame worked itself along. There were a couple of grenades still hanging on the belt, and I guess if they'd gotten hot enough they would have exploded and put me in a body bag too. But I didn't worry about that. I just sat there and watched the belt burn, fascinated by the way the fire moved along the tightly woven textile and left everything behind it black.

Honey followed my gaze, saw what was happening, and jumped into the foxhole and stamped out the fire. But I wasn't grateful. I was

just puzzled that the belt wasn't burning anymore.

Only three of our twelve tanks were able to return on their own power. So we left the others
behind and started the long hump back to C-2.
There was every reason to believe they'd follow
us and hit us again that night, so when we finally
stopped, no one was allowed to sleep. We stood
100 percent watch for two whole nights until we
limped into camp.

Then they let us sleep inside the camp perimeter for a couple of nights while the rest of
the companies stood watch, and I didn't really
think about Frenchy until the third day in. Then
I got some stationery and started a letter to Kay.

The death of a friend is always a shock, but in
combat it is both less traumatic and more so
than under normal circumstances. It is less traumatic because it is always half-expected. In the
wrong mood you look around you on a march
or drinking beer and think that some of these
guys are probably going to be dead soon. You
don't know which one, but after your eyes have
traveled around all the faces, you tell yourself:
"Well, it's going to be one of them—or else me."

In civilian life, on the other hand, 17-year-
old kids never think thoughts like that. They're
certain they'll never die, that somebody will in-
vent something and everybody will live forever;
or else they simply don't think about dying at
all.

So when somebody wraps a car around a
telephone pole and crushes his skull into a pulp,
it comes as a genuine shock. Suddenly you are

forced to look into the eyeless face of death—
something you weren't expecting to deal with, at
least until you were old and hump-backed and
ready to go.

On the other hand, there is a subtler and
slower shock that comes with losing a friend in
combat. In the first place, this guy is one of the
few companions you've got in the limited world
you inhabit. Nobody has more than two or three
close friends and no more than a dozen buddies.
When you lose one of these, your world is sub-
stantially diminished.

In civilian life you have your family—in
some cases literally hundreds of brothers, sisters, aunts, uncles, and cousins—as well as several circles of friends and close associates. If
you lose someone from one circle, you still have
a reservoir to draw on. But if you lose somebody
like Frenchy, you have one less good friend with
only a slim prospect that his replacement will be
somebody you like as well.

Also, every time you lose a friend in combat,
you have this sense that you are one step closer
to your own death, as if somehow it were fated
that he would go first, then you.

"It's me next," you tell yourself. "First him,
then me."

There's nothing particularly rational about
that kind of feeling, but everybody has it from
time to time. You brood for a day or two, maybe
drink a few extra beers for a few nights running,
and then shake it off. But when someone in your
company or platoon is killed, the feeling of fatal-
ity goes around like a flu bug. Everybody has it a
little, and a few people have it bad.

I had not been severely affected before, but

Frenchy was the closest thing to a good friend among those who had thus far died, and once I started thinking about him, I couldn't stop. He and I had been corresponding with the same girl, and now I was writing to say that he was dead. It could so easily have been the other way around.

But there was one other thing that bothered me. Though I was sorry Frenchy was dead, I wasn't as sorry as I probably should have been. I was too pleased to be alive and to have the knowledge that my own conduct during the crucial moments of battle had been more than adequate, that I had stood up to the ultimate confrontation and hadn't turned tail. I didn't think I was the world's greatest hero, but I thought I was okay.

That meant that I had come to the point where I had hoped to be when I first joined the Marines: I had seen the worst war had to offer, and I had been able to take it.

STAND-DOWN TIME

WITH FRENCHY, ROMEO, Manilla, and the new guy taken out in one day, I was the only one left on the machine gun team; so Blue sent out a call for replacements; and this time we got a couple of BNGs—Jim Lynch and Bob Mullins. We didn't get more, because the word came down that Al Manilla would be back in two or three weeks. I was relieved to hear it. The best way to replace a team in the field is one guy at a time, so that the newcomer feels he's working with veterans who know the ropes. Bring two new guys into a three-man or four-man gun team and you don't know what will happen. Lynch and Mullins seemed like they'd fit into Blue's platoon just fine, but you never knew till the bullets and the mortar shells started hitting.

Though I'd been in-country only a little over three months, I was now considered a seasoned veteran, largely because of the way I'd handled myself in the firefight on Mutter's Ridge. A few days after we'd returned from the Ridge, Redmon and Terry stopped by my bunk to talk to me. I could tell when they walked up that they had something on their minds.

"Hey, man," Terry said. "You did good back there. We think you got a medal coming."

Redmon agreed.

"I'm putting you in for a citation."

"Sounds great to me," I said.

About that time Blue popped into the barracks, and Redmon called him over.

"Sir, if it's okay with you, I'm going to put Herrod in for some kind of medal. Maybe a Bronze Star."

North shook his head.

"You can't do that," he said.

Redmon narrowed his eyes.

"Why not?"

"Because I've already put him in for the Navy Cross."

"Beats the hell out of a Bronze Star," Redmon said, and we all laughed.

I lay there a long time thinking about the medal. That's what we'd come for, at least the guys in this platoon; and I was glad to get one—particularly the Navy Cross, which was way up the ladder in decorations. Sometimes officers got medals for doing an especially good job in strategic planning. But enlisted men mostly got them for "bravery" or "gallantry" in action.

At the same time, the more I thought about it the more I realized that what I'd done was only what I'd been trained to do. At first I didn't go over to check on the machine gun because it was Manilla's job as team leader. But when it turned out he was wounded, then I went, shouting profanity all the way. I manned the machine gun because the gunner was wounded; and after I'd covered Lieutenant North until he'd regained consciousness, I'd started firing again because he'd ordered me to. And I kept on firing because

I wanted to kill the North Vietnamese before they killed me. Nothing extraordinary about all that. Just following Standard Operating Procedures, something Frenchy had probably done during the same firefight. But I got a medal and he got a plastic bag. So I was lucky. Still, I was happy about the citation, and it never occurred to me to turn it down.

I looked up and there was Ernie, a grin on his face, shaking his head. He'd heard.

"So how are you, Ira?" he asked.

"Ira?"

"Ira Hayes," he said. "You remember the 'Ballad of Ira Hayes.'"

I remembered all right. It had been a big hit record a while back—the saga of an American Indian who helped to raise the flag at Iwo Jima, a Congressional Medal of Honor winner.

"Knock it off," I said, and tried to get him to talk about something else, but from that time forward he called me "Ira." As it turned out, I wasn't awarded the Navy Cross, but I was approved for a Silver Star, which is the next best thing.

After that tough fight we lay around for a few days, but not for long. Before we knew it we were out on an ambush. It was daytime and we were staking out a trail that was commonly used by soldiers, but also by peasants as well, so we had to be careful about firing before we saw precisely who was out there.

Even near the DMZ, where we were fighting the North Vietnamese regulars rather than the Vietcong, it was difficult to distinguish civilians from soldiers, because often combat troops would dress up as peasant farmers, walk along rural roads, then suddenly pull out weapons and begin blasting away. Many a name now printed on that crooked wall in Washington belonged to a Marine who was bushwhacked by a grinning field worker with a rifle hidden under his peasant costume. For this reason we had to watch everybody very carefully. Sometimes we made mistakes—one way or the other—and either way the results were tragic.

Our machine gun team was positioned about 30 feet above a bend in the trail. Just down the road Ernie and his team were waiting in case the enemy got past. Suddenly we heard a noise behind us. No problem. It was Blue, who had come up to check our position. The sun was burning down from a cloudless sky, and for a moment when he stumbled I thought it might have been the heat. Then I looked again. One pants leg was soaked with blood.

We got a corpsman to take a look at him, and gradually I realized what had happened. When he'd gone down during the big firefight, he'd been hit in the legs by shrapnel. The wounds hadn't healed. We stood there and watched while Blue sprawled in a bomb crater and pulled his pants down. He had bleeding gashes in both legs and also in his butt. The dressings were clearly in need of changing, and one of the leg wounds had opened up.

"Did you report in after this happened?" the corpsman asked him.

"Forgot to," North said, and winced.

The corpsman grinned and began to peel the bandages away. Everyone knew that if Blue had turned himself in, he wouldn't have been allowed back in the field until the wounds healed. So he just hadn't mentioned it, not even to those of us who'd been next to him when he'd been knocked down. Though I admired him, I thought he was a little crazy. I'd have been happy to lie around for a couple of weeks, particularly after a firefight like that.

Finally the corpsman finished rebandaging the wounds, but before North could pull his pants back on, somebody whispered for us to be quiet, and then we saw them turning the bend—three Vietnamese, probably men, dressed in what looked like black pajamas and coolie hats. I slipped down behind the machine gun and began to sight them, and Mullins raised his M-14. The others drew a bead as well. But Lieutenant North held up a hand.

"Not yet. Not yet."

He took out the binoculars and peered at them as they walked along the path. We knew he was looking for rifles.

We were waiting to blow them away, but we watched Blue's raised hand as he continued to stare at the three walkers.

"Anybody see weapons?" he whispered.

We peered down. They were parallel to us now, so if they were carrying rifles in their right hands, the weapons would be shielded by their bodies.

Blue still stared through his binoculars.

"Hold it. Hold it. Not yet."

They began to turn the bend, but still Blue held us back.

"I still can't tell. Better let them go."

Unlike us, he remembered that the other

machine gun crew was just around the corner,
and he wasn't going to let us gun down three
unarmed civilians, even though he suspected—
as did we—that they were enemy soldiers dis-
guised as peasants.

We waited and listened. Silence. It sounded
as if they were going on through. Suddenly the
still air exploded, and we moved down as
quickly as we could, but we were too late. One of
the three had half his head torn off by machine
gun fire. Leroy Terry hit the second one in the
chest with a rocket, and all we could find of him
was tennis shoes and a hat. The third escaped.
But he had dropped his rifle, and two other rifles
were also lying on the path.

We had suspected them all along, but North
had made us wait. Despite his pain, he had carefully weighed the situation and, knowing we
weren't in any real danger, had given the three
walkers the benefit of the doubt. At the time, we
were eager for the kill. Later we talked about it
and decided he was right—but only because
we'd already seen what he was made of.

We pulled a lot of stand-down time after that. We
got our shots again. We got haircuts. We got
daily showers. We drank beer at night, and then
went to sleep inside the perimeter. We knew it
wouldn't last, but we didn't think about that. We
just enjoyed ourselves and raised a little hell.

One day Manilla showed up, almost healed,
ready to get back into action—as cocky as ever.
When he came into the bunker he took one look
at Jim Lynch and started shouting. So did
Lynch. As big a city as New York is, they'd gone

to the same high school and known each other well. So it was Old Home Week for the two of them. After a while some of the guys got a little sick of it, and told them to quiet down, but I understood how they felt. It was nice to talk to somebody who knew just how it looked and felt in your part of the country. We're all Americans; but in some respects we're different, if only because when we talk about America we're really talking about a particular patch of it, usually not more than fifty square miles. I had enjoyed talking to the mess sergeant from Oklahoma City, and I got a kick out of listening to Manilla and Lynch talk about the good-looking girls and the creeps in New York City.

Then Redmon came by one night and gave us the bad news.

"Blue's leaving the platoon," he said.

We were stunned.

"Why?" we asked.

"He's moving up to Executive Officer. We'll be getting another platoon leader, maybe in a week."

It wasn't so bad, because he would still be commanding us. But it wouldn't be the same.

"Hey, we can't call ourselves Blue's Bastards anymore," someone pointed out.

"We can't do that anyway," Redmon said. "They've just changed the brevity code. 'North' isn't 'blue' anymore. 'North' is now 'pine.' "

"So what will we be called now?"

"Some of the guys in the other outfits are already calling us 'Pine's Pansies,' " said Redmon.

"First guy calls me that," said Leroy Terry, "is gonna get his ass whipped."

We all agreed, though no one said it with quite the conviction that the Mighty T did.

"I think we should take up a collection and give Blue a going-away present," said Redmon. "Maybe a plaque."

"Where the hell could we get a plaque in this godforsaken country?"

"If everybody kicks in," said Redmon, "I'll guarantee to get the plaque."

Given his record, nobody could doubt that he would do it, so we all chipped in five bucks. And sure enough, a week later Redmon showed us the plaque, carved in the shape of a shield. It was made out of highly polished walnut and had a brass plate on it. On the plate were engraved the words: TO THE BIG BASTARD FROM ALL THE LITTLE BASTARDS.

That afternoon the platoon stood at attention in front of the bunker while Redmon presented the plaque to Lieutenant North. A few guys from other outfits were standing off to one side, wondering what the hell was going on, and Captain Goodwin, the company commander, was so curious that he came out of the officers' bunker wearing only his olive drab undershorts. He sat on the sandbag roof, while Redmon presented the plaque in behalf of all of Blue's Bastards, past and present. North grinned and so did we, but it wasn't entirely a joke, and we all knew it. Everyone did, that is, except Captain Goodwin.

After Blue accepted the plaque and made a few remarks, he turned to the Captain and threw him a smart salute. Instead of returning it,

Goodwin turned around, dropped his drawers, and mooned the lieutenant.

North turned around, grinning.

"Men," he said, "you've just seen the best side of the captain."

We moved back into combat slowly, like swimmers easing into a cold pool. We first started running squad sweeps out of C-2; and while there were a few enemy soldiers out there, most of them were the snipers who periodically fired rounds into the compound and then took off. But it was still dangerous, no matter where you were, as we immediately found out.

As we were moving over the flat landscape, we heard the sound of a Phantom jet and looked up, more out of habit than concern. We knew the sound in our sleep and couldn't have mistaken it for a MiG. The plane was swooping down, wiggling its wings, and all of a sudden we saw a bomb fly out and come hurtling down, straight at us. We hit the dirt, figuring we were already in body bags; but the bomb hit about 100 feet away, and I could feel the ground shaking under me from the concussion.

"What the hell was that for?" I shouted.

"I don't know," said Redmon, "but I'm sure as hell going to find out."

Blue was manning the radio, and he got on it immediately. Within a minute he was talking to the Phantom pilot while we listened, cheering Blue on. We were still shook, but it was almost worth the experience to hear North chew out the Air Force. He had a larger vocabulary for such conversations than we'd imagined.

A few minutes later he broke radio silence

to call us back in, and we were a little surprised. Maybe the incident was a little more important than we'd thought. When we got back to C-2, Blue was waiting for us with two Marine officers who looked grim-lipped and mean. So we figured there was trouble coming up. As we drew nearer, Ernie Tuten suddenly broke into a grin and started running.

"What the hell are you doing, Ernie?" I said. "Don't break ranks."

He ran straight to the two officers and started slapping them on the back, while North smiled. They were Ernie's brothers, and that night we all sat around in the bunker and drank beer with them, while we swapped stories. It was almost as if the war had stopped for a few hours and all bets were off.

As I sat there drinking, it occurred to me that it had been a strange day. Our own Air Force had tried to bomb us, and now a couple of officers were buying us beer. It was getting so you couldn't tell your enemies from your friends.

But all that ended in a couple of days, and we went humping back to Leatherneck Square (with North still in command of the platoon, since his replacement had not yet arrived). We ended up on hill 950 when the rain and fog rolled in; and while we weren't attacked by the enemy, there was no way the helicopters could resupply us. So we were socked in.

The days went by and we ran low on C-rations, even the ham and eggs. We didn't particularly like the food, but when we had our small portions cut in half, we began to feel the hunger.

"You know what I like . . ." somebody would say, and that would start it off. One by one we would recall some favorite meal and describe it in detail, while everybody else would listen and groan. It got to the point where no one could talk about anything else. If some North Vietnamese had accidentally stumbled into our command post we probably would have carved him up and roasted him on the spot.

At the height of this insanity I sat down and wrote a letter to my grandparents, telling them I was starving to death and listing all the things I wanted them to send me. I wrote the letter on toilet paper, and my list went on for almost five sheets.

Finally one morning we looked out to see that the fog had lifted, and shortly thereafter we heard the sound of the choppers, bringing us food—or so we thought. But they were actually there to fly us out, and we had to wait until we got back to get something to eat. We were unhappy until we heard where we were going: Razorback rather than C-2. We'd be getting real food for a while instead of C-rations. It was almost worth the wait.

A couple of weeks later word came for me to report to Lieutenant North at the duty hut. When I entered, he and Captain Goodwin were waiting for me.

"Herrod," said North, "do you see that 56-pound box?"

I looked and saw it. It was the biggest package I'd ever seen shipped through the U.S. mails, certainly the biggest I'd ever gotten.

"What's in there?" Captain Goodwin asked. "Your girl friend?"

I bent over and read the return address.

"It's from my grandparents," I said. "I guess it's food. That's what I asked for."

I hoisted it up on my shoulder and started out the door.

"I'll be around in a few minutes," North called after me, "and there'd better be something left."

The heck of it was, I wasn't really hungry anymore. Since we'd been back at Razorback we'd been eating three hot ones a day; and I had never been much for stuffing my gut, at least not in those days, so I wasn't all that excited.

But a lot of other guys were. When I opened it up I had an audience of about fifteen. I pulled out canned hams, boxes of cookies, candy bars, crackers, cheese, pickles, vegetables, two or three kinds of breads, mayonnaise, mustard, ketchup, fruit cocktail, apples, oranges, dried fruits, and even some popcorn. I think if I'd kept a copy of my list I could have checked it off and found everything I'd put down—and a couple of extras as well. I was grateful, but the time had passed when I would have been excited.

"Hey, Herrod," somebody said. "Why don't you start your own store?"

So I did, and for a few days I did a booming business, offering several kinds of sandwiches and almost any kind of snack food you could want—as long as it lasted. I even started to think about how I could order new stock, but I knew that every day we stayed at Razorback was a small miracle, and I didn't figure my grandparents would bite a second time.

* * *

Lynch and Mullins had become a part of the platoon at this point; and Mullins had gotten a lot of kidding because he was always falling asleep, particularly when the going got rough and we were under stress. Not only did he do it in the bunker and on choppers, but he was also dropping off in the field. I wondered what would have happened to Mullins if Blue had still been our platoon leader. The new lieutenant was still learning the ropes, and as yet he hadn't caught Mullins sleeping.

While we were at Razorback we still stood watch around the perimeter and put out our trip flares and Claymores every night. The strategy was simple but effective. The trip flares were triggered in the field by an advancing force or by a single infiltrator. They did no more than light up the landscape to show whoever was on watch how many people were out there. If it was no more than one or two, then you'd pick them off with a rifle or machine gun fire.

But if there was a large force moving up, then you would set off all the Claymores at once. They were our real insurance policy, and we always slept a little sounder at night, dreaming of North Vietnamese troops being torn to ribbons by thousands of hurtling steel balls. It was a hard system to penetrate, but sometimes the North Vietnamese were able to do it. So we still stood lines around the perimeter of Razorback, and our platoon was always part of the defense system.

But we hadn't encountered any enemy fire for weeks, and some of us were beginning to think that we'd have easy duty for the rest of the war. We still stood lines, of course, but most of us hung loose, except, of course, for the BNGs, who still peered out into the darkness and thought they saw shadows moving. Then it happened.

One night about 0200 hours, I was on watch in the fighting hole when suddenly the entire perimeter was lit with fire, and the earth almost came apart with the explosion. I had never heard anything like it. They were throwing something new at us this time. I studied the landscape in front of me, but all I could see was a shower of fading sparks. I didn't think anyone was out there, but I couldn't be certain.

Behind me men were shouting, and then there was an eruption of small arms and machine guns. Everybody was firing out into the darkness, so I set up the machine gun and started firing too. Then over the roar I heard someone shout, "Cease firing," and there was silence again.

A little later Redmon came over and told me what had happened: Mullins had been assigned to the hell-box, had fallen asleep, and had rolled over on the plunger. He'd set off every Claymore mine in the area and had sent thousands of little steel balls sailing harmlessly out into the night. When I heard about it I laughed, but it really wasn't funny anymore. Here was a guy who would be with us the next time we got in a firefight. How would he behave when an enemy force came charging up the hill? Would he fall asleep?

Over the next few days several of us tried to make him understand the dangers involved. He took our concern seriously and said it wouldn't happen again. Still it continued to bother me and a few of the others.

We didn't know it, but that night at Razorback was our last experience of stand-down time. The next day we piled the usual 80 pounds on our backs and boarded dusters for some sparrow hawking. The Army Corps of Engineers was building a road between Vandergriff and Razorback, and enemy snipers were doing everything they could to shut down construction. So we were going out there to wait for the enemy to attack, and then swarm all over him.

We were told we would be joined in the field by India Company, sent over from another sector; and after we'd bounced and rattled along for a few hours, sure enough, we saw tanks looming over the horizon on our right. When we intersected with them, we stopped for the day.

The snipers had probably seen us coming and pulled back. Our presence there gave the engineers a few uninterrupted days to do valuable work, but it also meant a large number of our tanks and two companies had been effectively removed from action by a handful of snipers. While we were there, pulling guard duty, nothing much happened.

And that was the real difficulty with the war —the fact that we weren't going anywhere or doing anything of significance. We were simply moving back and forth over the same territory, never advancing, never retreating. In World War II you could measure your progress in the Far East with each new island, and in Europe by the names of French and German towns. But over

here you went back and forth over the same terrain until you'd memorized every bomb crater
and every twisted stalk of elephant grass. You
went from C-2 to Leatherneck Square to Mutter's Ridge to Razorback to C-2 and then started
the cycle all over again. No matter how many of
the enemy you killed, you knew that you'd be
right at the same spot someday soon, and that
the next time they might kill you. You also knew
that you would never cross the DMZ but that the
enemy could cross it any time he wanted to.

So like the people back home, we felt a
sense of frustration that was always heightened
when we went out on dry runs like this one. As
we rode back on the dusters, we looked at one
another and shook our heads, the boredom
showing in our eyes. In a couple of days we
would have all the excitement we could handle
—and then some.

HUMPTY DUMPTY

HONEY CAME BY the fighting hole, shaking his head.

"What's wrong now?" I asked, barely interested.

"We're moving out, probably to the Ridge."

I felt immediately depressed. Every time we went up there we got hit. It was one of those exercises in futility that we'd learned to expect, maybe the worst, since no one was allowed to stay up there for long. I tried not to think about it, but fifteen minutes later the word came down the line: "Get ready to move out. The Ridge."

This time it was only Kilo Company. We were taken by chopper to the edge of the bush. Then, as usual, we humped it. Same old sand, same old elephant grass. Only when we started up the hillside did I feel any sense of uneasiness, and that was soon replaced by numbness. You didn't do this month after month without learning how to put your mind to sleep while your body marched on.

North came back to check on us and spoke to most of the platoon along the way. His manner hadn't changed a bit since he became executive officer. But his duties had. Now he was reponsible for the entire company. Because he was now leading the rest of the guys as well, they didn't give us such a hard time. Nobody called us Pine's Pansies, not with him gone and a new replacement as our platoon leader.

Our new platoon leader was with us such a short time I don't even remember his name. Nobody did. We called him "the new lieutenant" behind his back, and "sir" to his face. He'd had no combat experience; and though he was a good Marine officer, I figured we'd have to look after him rather than vice versa.

By evening we'd made it to the top of the Ridge, set up a command post, and formed a defense perimeter—a circle with foxholes about 15 or 20 feet apart. At Happy Hour we lay quietly in our foxholes and waited for all hell to break loose, but this time they surprised us. We heard nothing but the constant buzz of mosquitoes. We had our flak jackets on and we even tried bathing in G.I. mosquito repellent, but the Vietnamese mosquitoes craved the stuff. They'd come swarming all over you the moment you rubbed it on. Eventually we got used to being bitten, and we could sleep soundly while they lapped our blood. That night, with almost 200 of us up there, it must have been like Thanksgiving Day.

When the sky was totally black, we moved out, set up our trip flares and Claymores, and settled in for the night. I had to pull an early morning watch and was relieved by Mullins at 0300 hours; so before I'd hardly gotten back to sleep, it was dawn—morning, Happy Hour. For some reason I figured they'd be coming, so I kept awake instead of dozing and ate my Last Supper for breakfast. But I was wrong. No attack. Soon the sky was a pale blue, and everybody pinched off a little C-4, lit it, and began warming up cans of C-rations. I was beat, so I decided to catch a little sleep. I was just about to pull off my jacket when I heard the first one.

Thunk.

Somewhere, maybe five miles away, the enemy had dropped an 82-mm mortar shell into a tube, and we could hear it as clearly as if the guy in the next foxhole had fired it off. Suddenly there was a silence like nothing you ever heard. It was almost as if the birds knew what was coming.

Thunk.

We were the only unit in the area that day, so we knew the mortars were meant for us. What we didn't know was how well they had our coordinates, but we'd find that out very soon, because of the sound. If you heard a lot of whistling as the shell came toward you, then you were safe. If you heard a louder whistle that lasted no more than a split second, then you'd better duck, because it was coming in close.

Thunk.

But if you didn't hear anything, then you were dead, because no sound meant the whistle was behind the shell and it was curving right in on top of you, beating the sound by just the smallest part of a second. So it was the silence you really had to worry about.

Thunk.

That was the fourth one. Just after the fifth, the first round would arrive, and then for the better part of ten seconds you'd burrow down and hope you heard the whistle.

"Incoming!" Lieutenant North shouted from somewhere over to the left.

Thunk.

By then I was in mid-air, arriving in the foxhole a split second before I heard a short whistle and then the *kabloom* of the explosion. Another short whistle, another *kabloom.* An even shorter whistle, *kabloom.* Whistle, *kabloom.* Whistle, *kabloom.*

Never had the mortars hit so close. I held my hands under me, rolled into a ball, and tried to be all steel helmet. Already I was hearing *thunk, thunk* somewhere in the other side of the Ridge. They had us this time. There was no way out of the trap, unless we just turned and ran— but we knew half of us would be dead before we hit the downslope.

"Incoming!"

It was North again. Probably standing up, shading his eyes with his hands, jumping back half a second before the explosion.

Thunk.

Kabloom!

A short whistle this time, and in between explosions I heard somebody screaming.

"Jeez," said Lynch, "they've got our range. They've got us."

"Oh, God!" yelled somebody in the next foxhole, and four more explosions rocked the hillside.

"Corpsman!" somebody shouted. And then, *thunk, thunk.* The gooks had at least two mortars, maybe three. All we could do was hope they'd run out of rounds before we were all dead.

The explosions came split seconds after the

whistles, and each new series made it more and more obvious that they had our coordinates and knew it. They didn't even have to "walk it in" this time. They'd probably gotten tired of seeing us do the same thing every day and decided to do something different in response. So after we'd left the last time, they'd wasted a few mortar rounds zeroing in. Then they'd just sat there, waiting to see if we'd be stupid enough to come back to that same spot one more time. And we'd been just that stupid.

I heard loud screaming now, half in pain, half in terror. Somebody had been hit. But I didn't stick my head up to see, because already a new series was coming in on us, the *thunks*, the whistles, and the *kablooms* all intermixed with one another.

Someone else was screaming now, calling for a corpsman again. Later I found out what had happened. The first corpsman had run over to a guy who'd been trapped outside, heard the next round coming, and thrown himself over the wounded man to protect him from the flying shrapnel. The round had landed right between their legs and blown them both into several pieces.

It was for just such occasions that the Marines made us wear two sets of dog tags, one around our necks, the other laced into one boot. If your head got blown off they could always figure out who you were by checking your foot. If your foot was missing, they hoped to hell you still had your head. It was only in heavy artillery or mortar fire that you were likely to be blown into so many pieces that you were Humpty

Dumpty. Well, we had a few Humpty Dumpties that day.

They were dropping shells right into the foxholes, and as we cringed there, praying they'd stop, we knew just how close they were hitting. There were screams and groans from all over the Ridge, and the rounds kept coming, one series after another, sometimes with no more than ten seconds in between.

At one pause I quickly stuck my head up, then ducked down immediately. But I was sorry I had done it. The second I stayed up, my gaze went right to a pile of raw hamburger, hanging out of a foxhole. Whoever that had been had never heard the whistle and would never hear anything else.

For a moment I panicked. I didn't think I could stand another second, much less the twenty minutes or an hour it would probably take them to exhaust their ammunition. Somewhere behind me I heard Captain Goodwin shouting into the telephone. He'd be calling in an air strike on the enemy, and choppers for the dead and wounded. It occurred to me that if I got wounded I could be medevacked out, otherwise I was certain that we'd all be killed. Without considering the matter for long, I decided I was willing to get my arm blown off.

So on the fifth *thunk* I threw my right arm in the air, realized in an instant what I'd done, and hauled it down just as quickly. That was the arm I'd need to write and feed myself and do a hundred other things. No need to sacrifice that one when I still had a left arm.

On the next series I threw up my left arm, hoping for a piece of shrapnel big enough to make a hole, but small enough to leave me some use of my hand. However, my arm led a charmed life. It waved up there for ten or twelve series without getting a scratch. Finally I got a muscle cramp and pulled it back down.

After about twenty minutes of continuous shelling, we heard the Phantoms, but we couldn't even manage a cheer. We could tell from the screams and shouts that we'd already lost a bunch of guys. If we were lucky, the Phantoms would spot the mortar teams and send twenty or thirty rockets right into their faces. A good fighter pilot could literally hit a man if he could get him in his sights. The trouble was, the mortar teams knew all too well the Phantoms would be coming, so they would try to camouflage themselves and continue firing. Sometimes they got away with it, sometimes they didn't. This time they got away with it, though they were slowed down from time to time. Meanwhile, two choppers filled with corpsmen landed just down the slope on level ground. They came running up the hill with blood, stretchers, and body bags; and just as they gained the crest of the Ridge, another series came roaring in and Humpty Dumptied one of them, the second corpsman we'd lost in a matter of minutes.

They tended to the wounded first, then came back and scraped their buddy into a body bag and got the rest of ours as well. During the lulls we'd poke our heads out for a few seconds. I counted nine or ten body bags hauled off toward the choppers, and later I learned that we'd lost eighteen or twenty, depending on whether or not you counted the corpsmen.

There were guys with arms and legs torn

away, feet missing, guts hanging out. And the corpsmen cleaned them up and stuffed them in bags, the way you'd gather up spilled garbage— quickly, mechanically, without looking at what you were doing or risking a deep breath. Of course they were in a hurry. After they'd carried off the wounded, they did stop to dive in a fox- hole every time a round came whistling in, but they knew the sooner they bagged the bodies, the sooner they'd be able to haul their own rear ends onto the choppers. It was a dangerous and grim job they did, but as one of the choppers took off, for the first time I envied them.

It's difficult to describe continuing terror. You can tell what prompted it in the first place, and then all you can do is repeat yourself. But when you live through it for two hours—as we did that morning—it never gets monotonous, or even less frightening. You always know that guys are getting rounds dumped into their laps the whole while and that the next round may be the silent one that gets you—after an hour of dodging, just when you think you've made it.

So we all crouched and shivered in terror. Then, after constant bombardment, there was si- lence for two or three minutes, and suddenly I heard Captain Goodwin shout in a hoarse voice, "Okay, men, let's get off this goddamned Ridge. Move out!"

When we got back to C-2 we slept for a couple of days; but this time we didn't sleep so soundly.

When I was in high school I had boxed a little, but I never was particularly good at it. I fought a few fights, won some and lost some, but I was

always better at basketball and baseball. Still, I
liked the sport and missed it. I'd always had
guys to spar with back home, but nobody in the
platoon was interested, not even Leroy Terry,
who had been a professional wrestler and who
could have torn my head off if he'd landed a
solid punch. Then I heard that one of the guys in
the outfit had been a top boxer in college—Lieutenant Oliver North.

So the next time I saw him I brought it up.

"How about going a few rounds with me,
sir."

He grinned.

"Sounds great. You think we could find any
gloves?"

Of course he was right—there wasn't any
equipment like that around.

"How much boxing did you do?" I asked.

"Quite a bit," he said. "It was an important
sport at the Academy, and I liked it."

I told him about my fights, my weaknesses,
went into a few details, and he told me about
some of the bouts he'd fought. He wasn't reluctant to talk, but he was matter-of-fact in what he
told me. No tall tales. No boasting. At the same
time there was no false modesty either. He
didn't say how bad he was and then give you
examples to the contrary. The way he told me
about it, you would have thought he was talking
about somebody else. But I could tell that he really loved the sport and had put a lot into it.

"What was your biggest fight?" I asked.

He shrugged his shoulders.

"I guess for the championship of the Naval
Academy."

"No kidding?" I said.

"Yeah, it was a big deal at the time. Everybody came. Lots of bets. The guy I was fighting had it all over me. He was bigger. Had the reach. Was a better boxer. So I guess he was the favorite. But somehow he'd never won the big ones, so I had a few guys who were betting on me."

"Who won?" I asked.

"I beat him," he said simply.

He told me some of the story that day, and much later I filled in more of the details after reading some published accounts of his life. He had beaten his opponent out of sheer determination, rushed him off his feet from the opening round to the last bell, kept swinging, never gave up. He'd won because he'd refused to quit—a quality that made him a good commander in the field.

Recently I read an interview with North in which he was quoted as saying, "Sometimes a battle is not won by strategy. It's won by some stupid platoon leader saying, 'Let's go up that hill.' " The quote reminded me of the fight at Annapolis and of the kind of leadership he provided for us in Vietnam. When he told his men to take a hill, he went first; and because he thought we could fight and win, we thought so too.

When he told me that story almost twenty years ago he was a lieutenant, and no one except his family, friends, and his platoon knew who he was. I don't remember whether or not he gave me the name of the man he fought. Certainly I would never have heard of him, since he would have been no more than a lieutenant himself. Years later, when I was interviewed by *Life*, I remembered the story he'd told me about the championship fight and passed it along to the reporter. Someone checked the details and came up with the name of North's opponent and his current whereabouts. He was James Webb, and at that time he was Secretary of the Navy. Somewhere along the line he must have won a few big ones.

In a day or two we were back on the march and into more trouble, though this time it was not the North Vietnamese. The problem lay within our own ranks.

I was sound asleep, stretched out on the side of the hill, when suddenly I felt a heavy pressure on my chest and somehow I knew in an instant it was a boot. Blinking and staring up into the darkness, I saw a familiar face and felt relief. It was a black face, and it belonged to the corporal of the guard. He kept his boot on my chest and increased the pressure slightly, as he bent over.

"Who's on watch?" he whispered.

"What time is it?" I asked.

"0330 hours," he said.

I thought.

"Mullins," I said.

He took his foot off my chest and rolled his eyes.

We moved quietly through the night to where Mullins was supposed to be keeping watch, and when I first saw him sitting there, bent over his rifle, I thought he was awake. Then I noticed the closed eyelids and the tremble of his lower lip as he exhaled.

"I'll take care of this," I told the corporal of the guard, and he nodded and disappeared. We both understood the seriousness of what had happened.

I shook Mullins awake, and he started to apologize, but I held up my hand.

"Don't bother," I said. "It's not your fault. But you can't stay here. It's too dangerous for all of us. You're going to be medevacked out tonight."

His eyes widened. No one was medevacked unless he was seriously ill or wounded.

"How?" he asked, now fully awake.

"You're going to break something," I told him. "I'll let you choose what you break. Arm, leg, or jaw? Take your pick."

He stared straight ahead for a long moment, and I was afraid he was going back to sleep. Then he nodded his head.

"Okay," he said. "I'll take the leg."

I shook my head, thinking he'd made a poor choice, and looked around for something to use as a fulcrum. Nearby I saw a stump.

"Come over here," I said. "Lay your leg on this stump and I'll break it with the butt of my rifle."

He followed me over to the stump, his face a little whiter than usual. With a sigh he lay down and propped his leg up on the stump. When I rammed that nine-pound rifle into his shin he gasped, but he didn't cry out. The bolt rattled so loudly the gooks must have heard it on the other side of the mountain, but the bone didn't crack. So I rammed it again, leaning into the rifle with all my weight. Still no break.

"Put your arm up there," I whispered. "The leg's too big."

Because the bolt on the rifle rattled, I tried

my steel helmet this time, but when I clobbered
him on the arm it sounded like a Chinese gong,
and I concluded there was no way I would be
able to break the arm either.

"I'm sorry," I said. "But it's going to have to
be your jaw."

He hesitated, but he knew he had no choice;
so he dragged himself to his feet and stood there
while I set his jaw at just the right angle. Then I
wound up and threw a haymaker. I'll say this for
him: he didn't flinch, and I caught him right on
the point of his chin. He reeled against me spitting blood, only half conscious. After we'd both
examined ourselves, he confirmed that his jaw
was broken; and I discovered that my hand was
broken as well.

"Okay," I whispered, "you were walking
along, fell into the foxhole, and cracked your
jaw on the butt of the M-60. Got that?"

He nodded with a glazed look in his eye,
and I went off to get the lieutenant. He returned
with me, took one look at Mullins's jaw, and sent
him off to find a corpsman. Then he turned to
me, eyes narrowed.

"I know you broke his jaw, Herrod, so how
did it happen?"

For an instant I started to tell him, but I
knew it would involve too much red tape for everybody, and in the end nothing would be
changed, so I just shook my head.

"Like he said, he fell and hit his jaw on the
machine gun."

"Hold out your hands," said the lieutenant.

I held them out thinking that my right one
was too numb to hurt yet, but I was wrong.
When the lieutenant squeezed both hands I

thought I'd scream with the pain; and when he started kneading them, sweat broke out on my brow. But I clenched my teeth and tried to look him straight in the eye. Finally he dropped my hands and shook his head.

"I can't prove anything, Herrod, but I know you did it. We'll have him medevacked out first thing in the morning."

I gave him a quick nod and reeled off into the darkness, throbbing with pain. Then next morning, just at daylight, a chopper came angling down onto the hillside and two corpsmen picked up the stretcher Mullins was strapped in and carried it to the plane, while I waved goodbye to him with my left hand.

By then my right hand was as big as a catcher's mitt and about as useless. I knew I wouldn't be any good in a fight, and I wasn't sure I'd be able to stand the pain much longer. I thought about the situation for a while and finally decided there would have to be a second accident. But I couldn't just run up to the lieutenant and tell him I'd hurt my hand. He would know something was fishy. I'd have to have the accident in front of him.

The sooner the better, so I looked around and found him, talking to some guy in a foxhole. I ambled up, started to ask him something, lost my balance, and tumbled into the foxhole on top of the poor guy already in there.

"You okay, Herrod?" the lieutenant asked, peering down at me.

"Well, I don't know, sir," I said. "I seem to have hurt my hand."

* * *

They didn't medevac me out, the way they did Mullins. Shortly after I'd gone through my act, we got orders to pull back to C-2; and even though my hand was blue and swollen, the lieutenant decided I could wait another day and go back with the rest. So I ate aspirin and managed to keep from crying out from the pain as we walked back down the hillside.

Later, when I was having my hand wrapped in a cast, I heard the news.

"You in the outfit with that fellow Mullins?" the medic asked.

I nodded, on guard despite the pain.

"Lucky guy. It'll take him a couple of months for that jaw to heal. He's been flown back to the States. War's over for him."

As the medic finished up the job, I thought about Mullins, with all the time in the world to sleep now, and I was glad for everybody's sake. Then it occurred to me that since he was no longer under any pressure, he probably would be wide awake for the rest of his life.

For days the newspapers had been full of reports that the 3rd Marines would be pulling out of Vietnam. President Nixon had promised a reduction of forces, and this was to be the fulfillment of that promise. Though some of us had become addicted to battle, we still hated Vietnam and were ready to go back home—so we were watching and waiting to see what happened.

Some guys had already written home about it and were making plans to be met on the West Coast by their families. I hadn't gone that far, but I had talked a lot about the probability and was ready to move out. Then it was official. President Nixon had done what he said he would do. The 3rd Marines had been ordered back home. We broke out our hoarded beer and were in the process of holding a party when somebody came out to the perimeter and told us the grim truth: it was all a lie.

The 3rd Marines were going back all right. There would be a band waiting at the dock. The troops would march off, and the press would be there to cover it. But the only people who would get off would be the short-timers and the standard bearers carrying the colors. The rest of us —ninety percent of the 3rd Marines—would still be in Vietnam. We were being transferred to the 1st Marines.

Instead of a celebration, we had a wake. We were not only staying in Vietnam—we were going to be broken up. That would be the end of Blue's Bastards.

When Lieutenant North came by a little later, we stopped him and asked what was going to happen. He confirmed what we'd heard.

"You'll be going to the 1st Marines."

We noticed the way he put it.

"Where will you be going, sir?"

He smiled.

"Back to the States."

We were glad for him, but nobody could conceive of serving without him. He had held us together and given us a sense of our own invincibility. Somehow we knew that while we ourselves were vulnerable and might well be killed as the result of an accident or some mistake on our own part, we never believed for a second that our platoon or our company could be wiped out. Now anything was possible. We looked at each other in frustration, and maybe in fear. I couldn't tell what the others were thinking or feeling. But I knew that somehow my attitude would not be the same again, that in some real sense my second tour of duty in Vietnam was beginning, and I liked the thought of it less than when I'd first landed in Saigon. It had been bad enough, even serving under North. Now it was going to be worse, though how much worse I didn't know.

We sat around for a while on the perimeter, thinking about what we could do; and when nobody came up with a better idea, we decided to have a party. We all chipped in for refreshments, and Redmon was delegated to get the beer, whisky, and whatever else was available.

We had the party the night before Blue took off for Saigon and then the States, and he came by and joined us for a while. A platoon is around 50 men, so naturally we broke up into smaller groups and reminisced about the things that had happened, and the guys we had known who were gone by then. Not the ones who were killed. If their names came up at all it was by accident. It may have been superstition and it may have been a way of dealing with our own continuing risk; but we talked about them as if they were no more than incidental figures in our lives, people who had come and gone in a day or an hour. Later at the Vietnam Memorial I would remember them all, in one rush of emotion, sitting down on the sidewalk in Washington, D.C., and crying for what must have been thirty minutes. But that night we were determined to have a good time and to be a platoon for one more hour, because the next day we would be serial numbers on our way to new assignments.

Lieutenant North came around to every group and talked with us, recalling incidents, kidding, trying to make us feel as if things had not come to an end, though most of us concluded that they had. I don't remember for sure, but I think somebody asked him to say a few words. Otherwise I don't believe he would have done anything to make the situation more painful than it already was.

He talked a little bit about the accomplishments of the platoon, though not more than a few sentences, then he said the one thing that could have made a difference under such circumstances.

"Men, I want you to know that I'm proud to have served with you."

We echoed what he had said. Then he was gone.

There was no melodrama in all of this. He could have made a long speech, wrung us like wash rags, but he didn't. Yet it would be difficult for anyone else to appreciate just how we felt after those few words. I don't believe there's anything quite like the bond that men who have fought together feel. There is a sense in which you are closer to such men, even the ones you don't like, than you are to your best friend or even your wife.

And the best thing you can say about one another, the only real measure of what you are, is that you were a good man to fight beside.

So it meant a lot to those of us who admired Lieutenant North to hear him pay us that particular compliment. And he meant it, too. You could tell it in the words he used and the way he looked when he said them. It would help to carry us through the next days of reassignment, and then we would be in a new unit and starting all over.

Of course, I didn't realize it then, but I would see Blue again; and in this respect I would be unique among everybody else in the bunker that night. But the circumstances under which I saw him would not prompt anybody else to envy me or to want to change places. In the citation he wrote recommending me for a medal, he said that I had shielded him with my own body, at risk to my own life. I suppose I did, though I didn't think about it at the time.

But one thing is certain—when he returned to Vietnam to save my life, it was with full knowledge of the sacrifice he was making; and I'm certain that he came without thinking twice.

PART

TROUBLE IN THE SOUTH

THE FIRST THING I heard about the fighting in the south was bad news. A sergeant who had been stationed with the 1st Marines shook his head when I asked him about the outfit. We were drinking beer in Quang Tri, just before I shipped out, and he was the only person I could find who had already been where I was going.

"It's not only the people you have to watch out for down there," he told me, shaking his head grimly. "Up here at least you got a chance, because you're fighting something human. But down there it's another matter."

I watched him as he talked, trying to gauge whether or not he was putting me on; but he seemed to be serious.

"You never know when you'll run into them damn booby traps," he continued. "The Vietcong will slip right into camp and wire anything and everything. If you see a Coke can you don't dare kick it because your leg might be blown off. You'll never know when you'll stumble over a wire and see your arms and legs go flying in five different directions. I'd rather be in a firefight any day."

He took a big gulp of beer and frowned at me.

"And they're geniuses at picking up our old ordnance and using it against us. They'll take a five-hundred-pound bomb, a two-hundred-fifty-pound bomb, three or four hand grenades, and a few mortar rounds and string them together in a daisy chain. You'll be walking through a field, one guy will trip over all this jerry-rigged stuff, and you'll lose ten guys in a split second. You've got to realize that these people have been practicing this kind of warfare for twenty years, starting with the French forces."

I should have gotten up and left right then, but instead I ordered another round and listened to more of his talk.

"You're fighting guerrillas—men, women, even children. They farm by day. You see them out there, bent over, rooting around in the ground. They grin and wave at you, and you think they're the friendliest people in the world. Then, after the sun goes down they turn into terrorists."

"Why?" I asked. "Who are they?"

"The Vietcong? Nothing but a bunch of communists. Or people under communist influence. Their orders are to make our presence in this country as difficult and as dangerous as possible, and they do a damn good job of it. They operate all around you. In the middle of you. They sabotage. They murder. And you never do know who the hell they are, because civilians are all around you."

I shrugged my shoulders and tried to act nonchalant, but he had gotten to me. Later that night I ran into a couple other guys, and they said the same thing. Of course, I knew how good it made some guys feel to say they'd already been through the same hell you were just about to face. I'd run across that attitude in boot camp, so I shouldn't have let it bother me—but I did. Part of my panic came from a growing realization that I was on my own now. My buddy Ernie Tuten had been shipped in another direction, and so had the other guys. But most important— I wouldn't be serving under Lieutenant North.

Let's face it. I was nineteen years old and scared out of my senses. I had been fairly independent by the time I got out of high school and even a little rebellious, but I wasn't really able to go out into the world and stand on my own two feet. I was physically a man, and I was emotionally mature in many ways. But I still had some growing up to do; and while being a member of Blue's Bastards had helped me bridge the gap between being a kid in a family and an independent adult, I soon discovered that somewhere in a dark corner of me there was a big baby, ready to start crying when things didn't go his way.

So despite the beers I had drunk that night, more than I could remember, I lay awake thinking until a cold sweat broke out on my forehead and I sat up in bed, staring into the darkness in terror. I decided at that moment that I couldn't handle going to the 1st Marines, where I figured I'd get fragmented into a bunch of chicken parts by a booby trap.

I also knew that some of what was bothering me was a lack of confidence in officers and NCOs I had never met, a platoon I hadn't even joined. Blue had looked out for us. Who would be doing that now? And it wasn't just physical

fear. It was fear of the unknown. The more I
thought about it, the more I choked inside.

So I decided to go AWOL.

Since my arm was still in a cast, I was first
sent to NSA, a hospital in Da Nang, where I got
an X ray. The doctors said my hand was healed,
took off the cast, and concluded I was fit for
duty. When I walked out the door I declared myself temporarily free from all obligations to Marines and country and resolved to float for a
while, then make up my mind what to do. In my
heart I knew that eventually I would go back,
but I did consider alternate plans—hiding out in
Vietnam till the end of the war, finding some
way to get back to the States, joining some other
unit under an assumed name.

While I thought about all these possibilities,
I tried to be as inconspicuous as possible, to
move around from place to place, to avoid being
questioned. There were several military bases
around the city as well as some great R-and-R
facilities, so I would find a place where one of
the Bastards had been reassigned, get him to
find me a spare bunk, hang around for a couple
of days, then go visit somebody else. If the guy
was pulling duty during the day, then I would
find an R-and-R center and shoot pool until he
got off in the afternoon. If he was pulling night
duty, I'd move around with him all day, then
sleep in his bunk at night.

The best place to hang out was the China
Beach U.S.O., one of the biggest R-and-R centers
in Vietnam, though it was really no more than a
club surrounded by a bunch of hooches. Occasionally somebody would come around to check

orders, but it was easy enough to avoid them if
you just kept your eyes open.

For a while it seemed like a great life. Then I
ran out of money. Though I could always find a
chow line to join and an empty bunk to sleep in,
I had to give up some of the basic necessities—
like beer and women.

Then, too, I had never been happy with my
decision to go AWOL; and after a while I realized
that eventually I'd have to go back, that the
longer I delayed, the worse the punishment
would be when I turned myself in.

Finally I made up my mind. I was lounging
around Freedom Hill, an R-and-R center with a
movie theater, a PX, and a beer garden—none of
which I could enjoy, because I was flat broke.
Suddenly the futility of what I was doing hit me,
and in an instant I knew what I had to do.

"To hell with this," I said out loud, got up,
and walked into the headquarters there at the
center.

The commanding officer looked up as I
walked in, and I think he probably knew just
why I was there. Apparently guys turned themselves in almost every day.

"What can I do for you?"

"I'm AWOL," I said. "I want to be sent back
to my unit."

He nodded his head.

"Just sit down right there. We'll take care of
you."

He picked up the phone and began to dial
what was obviously a familiar number.

"How long have you been AWOL?" he asked,
as he waited for someone to answer.

"Two months," I said.

* * *

An MP delivered me to headquarters, where my
new platoon commander was waiting for me in
his office. He was a Lieutenant Lewis, a black
man who was six feet two and weighed about
two hundred pounds. He already had my file on
his desk, and he opened it while I stood before
him at attention. I later learned that he'd been a
chief petty officer, teaching combat tactics on a
transport bringing BNGs to Vietnam. He'd been
in combat himself and knew his subject well
enough to attract the attention of a Marine general, who'd recommended him to Quantico,
where he came out an officer—and one of the
best.

After a minute or two he shook his head and
told me to stand at ease.

"Herrod," he said, "you've got a good record
here. What happened?"

I told him exactly what I'd done and why I'd
done it.

He glanced back down at my file.

"You've got good reports from your company commander. Good reports from your platoon leader. Silver Star recommendation. You
should have reported on time and then talked to
me about your problems. You didn't have to go
AWOL."

"Yes, sir," I said. "I know that now."

"You still worried about those booby traps?"

"A little. Not as much."

I saw the first trace of a smile.

"Well, it's good to worry a little."

Then he was all business again.

"Okay. You report to the first sergeant while
we see what we need to do."

* * *

I waited around for several days, wondering what would happen, hoping I wouldn't draw time in the brig. But I later found out that Lieutenant Lewis was doing everything he could to avoid a court-martial. He was making calls, trying to get some kind of ruling that would allow him to handle my case at the company level. He didn't want a conviction on my record.

However, I'd been gone too long, so I was given a summary court-martial, the lowest level of disciplinary action that involves a trial. The punishment a summary court-martial could hand out was limited, and no one raised an eyebrow when they saw it on your record. Plenty of guys had gotten a summary court-martial for getting drunk and beating up on their buddies.

But I did get my own lawyer and my own judge. My lawyer was Captain Williams, a tall, thin black officer who looked like he'd been on a hunger strike. He had a dry wit and a friendly manner; and I trusted him as soon as he began to talk, because I realized he was more like a civilian defense lawyer than a career Marine. I had a feeling he would do anything it took to win my case.

As I told him my story, he listened intently, then nodded.

"Sounds goo-o-od," he said. "Decorated hero. Good combat record. Never ran in battle. Before we're through they'll be giving you a medal for running off."

Then he laughed so hard that pretty soon I was laughing too.

I didn't do quite as well as he had predicted; but I did okay. I admitted I was guilty, pled extenuating circumstances, and Captain Williams laid it on thick when he told the judge about my record. The judge, Captain Lucy, listened to the story, made notes, then looked at me.

"Did you intend to return eventually, or did you plan to hide out forever."

"I pretty much knew I would eventually report in," I said. "I just wasn't ready."

"Are you ready now?"

"Yes, sir," I said. "I won't do it again, if that's what you mean."

He nodded and made a few notes.

"I'm going to take this case under advisement," he said. "When I'm ready to render a judgment, I'll let you know."

He rose, and we both snapped to attention.

"What do you think?" I asked Captain Williams after we'd left the courtroom.

"I think they'll probably shoot you," he said.

Captain Lucy called us back into the courtroom later that day, and I stood at attention while he read me my sentence in a quiet, matter-of-fact tone.

"Three months at hard labor, a three-months' fine of $70 per month, and reduction in rank from E-3 to E-1."

I'd expected to be busted from lance corporal to private, but I hadn't expected to be pulling time in the brig.

"The three months at hard labor is probated," he added, and I felt a lot better.

So that was it. I was told to report to the company first sergeant for reassignment. When I'd first come over to Vietnam I'd been making $42.50 a month; and even with the reduction, I'd be making more than that, once the fine was paid off. As for the rank, who thought about rank in the field? The truth was, I didn't really care, just so long as I didn't have to pull hard time in the brig.

But when I went to the duty hut to talk to the first sergeant, I really got a shock. He looked up, smiled, and said, "Herrod, you want to go on R-and-R leave?"

His name was Lloyd, and he was a big man with graying brown hair and a gentle but firm manner. The day I'd first reported to the company, I'd spent a lot of time in the duty hut, and we'd had an opportunity to talk. He was a good listener, and we got along well from the start. It occurred to me that he might well have been responsible for the company commander's attitude in all this. Still, what he was offering now seemed beyond belief.

I reminded him that I'd just gotten back from R-and-R, but he didn't seem to hear me.

"How would you like to visit Sydney, Australia?"

I told him that Sydney would do just fine.

Then he looked me straight in the eye.

"If I let you go, will you come back?"

I hesitated for just an instant, because I knew he was asking me to give my word.

"Yeah," I told him. "I'll come back."

"In which case," he said, "I'll get the orders cut."

I was happy for about ten minutes until I realized that I didn't have any money left. The flight to and from Australia would be courtesy of the U.S. government, but the drinks and the Australian women would have to be paid for out of my own pocket. I thought about it a while, then decided to call my grandparents and borrow a little money. Once I got back I'd be in the field and wouldn't need it anyway.

My grandfather said he'd wire the cash, provided I went to the places he remembered from World War II.

"I want to know if everything is still the same. You go, then write me a letter about it."

I told him he had a deal.

I was sitting in the Saigon airport, watching television, when I saw a pair of flame red slacks go by, stop, then come back. I didn't have to look up to find out who was wearing them, because I was sure I knew. I'd seen them in the U.S. at Staging Battalion—slacks with a color like none I'd ever encountered before, worn by Al Hafer of Myrtle Beach, S.C. I'm sure that there were other pairs of red slacks in Vietnam, but none quite that shade of flame red.

Sure enough, I looked up and there was Hafer, grinning at me, his hand outstretched. He was a tall, fair-haired guy who talked with what he said was a South-Carolina-Low-Country accent. We'd been good friends at Staging Battalion; and better yet, he was on his way to Sydney for a week of R-and-R—just like me. So we decided to stick together and see the sights.

We stayed at the Hotel Australia in the King's Cross area of Sydney, because we'd heard that section of town was one big party; and sure enough, it was. After we'd checked into the hotel we showered and shaved, then hit the sidewalk, ready for action. It was twilight—Happy Hour—

and as we looked down the street we saw nothing but neon lights advertising bars. It looked a little like the pictures of Las Vegas.

"I'll tell you what," said Hafer. "Let's start out by drinking one drink at every bar on the block."

I thought that sounded like a good idea, so we walked a few steps and hit the first night spot. Early the next morning when we reeled back to our room, we'd barely begun, and after a week of highly conscientious bar hopping we weren't halfway down the block. We concluded that there wasn't a better nightclub strip in the world.

It is strange how the isolation of war affects men. We had both been living in the field for months, moving around in a maze of tents and barracks, sleeping in foxholes or bunkers, bathing in streams, eating in mess halls or out of cans. As a consequence, when we went into a restaurant we suddenly felt out of place and ill at ease. As we sat down at a table that first night, both of us had the same sense of being onstage.

"Why is everybody staring at us?" Hafer asked me.

"I don't know," I said, "but we're doing something wrong."

I looked around as nonchalantly as I could; and while no one was looking at that precise moment, I was certain they'd been staring just a second earlier. If Hafer had been wearing his red slacks I would have understood what was happening, but he was wearing what everyone else was wearing.

We'd ordered shrimp; and when they came, we each picked up one and dipped it in tartar sauce. At that moment it seemed as if the whole room bent forward.

"Hell," said Hafer, "I'm going to cut mine up with a knife."

"I guess I will, too," I said, and we both carved around on the shrimp for an hour, while everyone in the place seemed to watch every bite. It wasn't until two or three days had passed that we felt comfortable in civilization again. It was a strange feeling, and I'll never forget it.

Needless to say, we were looking for girls as soon as we got off the plane; and we finally figured out an easy way to meet them. Nothing is more innocent looking than a sightseer with a camera, so we took my camera, removed the film, and then went out on the streets, looking for girls. When we'd see one, we'd ask her to pose for us, just so people back in the States could see how good-looking Australian women were. Most of them were friendly, and we would try to strike up a conversation with them afterwards. We met bunches of girls that way.

The last day I was there I decided to go out and take the sightseeing tour for my grandfather. Mostly what I was supposed to visit were historic buildings and landscaped parks, so I bought a fifth of Wild Turkey, hired a cab, and gave the driver a list of the stops I had to make. Then I sat back and concentrated on the whisky. At some point I guess one place began to look pretty much like another; but I didn't care, because I was having a great time watching the world spin round and round the cab. Eventually it was spinning so fast I forgot that I had to go back to Vietnam, and I thought about just getting out of the cab and disappearing forever into all those great clubs along the strip.

But the next morning I remembered I'd made a promise to Sergeant Lloyd, so I got another bottle, opened it on the way to the airport, and when I came back to my senses we were landing in Saigon.

When I went back into the field, I found out that although LZ Ross, the Fire Support Base where we were stationed, was only 26 miles south of Da Nang, we were fighting an entirely different war from the one we fought around the DMZ. Our enemies, the Vietcong, were guerrillas who used terrorist tactics to harass and demoralize us. Since most of them farmed by day, the fighting was almost always at night, and we did not use orthodox tactics ourselves.

Instead of being divided up into squads and machine gun teams all the time, we would usually go out in "killer teams." These were really five-man roving ambushes, using what the manual called "counter-insurgency tactics." We would go out under cover of darkness, set up ambushes along known trails, and wait for someone to fall into the trap. If the enemy showed up, we would hit, then run—unless one of our party was wounded. Only then would we stick around to fight it out and wait for reinforcement at daylight. We were equipped with a radio and M-16 rifles, but hardly ever with machine guns, mortars, or rocket launchers.

In effect we were out there in the darkness doing to the Vietcong what they were doing to us —but with a couple of exceptions. First, we took prisoners and all they did was kill. Second, we had rules by which we were supposed to play and they didn't. One of the Articles of Engagement stated that you could not fire on a person in civilian clothes unless he fired on you first, even if he had a weapon in his hand. That particular restriction imposed greater restraints on us than most American police departments operated under, and it was apparent to our field officers that you just couldn't fight a war that way —not if you wanted your men to survive.

So we would modify the rules slightly when we got in a tight spot. If a civilian had a weapon and gestured in your direction, you got off a round as quickly as you could, whether or not he'd fired. As we used to say, "Whoever gets it up first lives the longest." It was like a gunfight in a Western movie; you just had to have witnesses that the other guy drew first. The Cong, of course, had no such rules governing their conduct. They could kill an American fighting man under any circumstances, whether or not he was armed; and they took the easiest and safest route if they could—booby traps, sniping from a hidden position, coming up behind you and slitting your throat.

While Lieutenant Lewis assigned me to a machine gun team so he would have the platoon organized by the book, I was really part of a killer team and as soon as the trial was over I went back into the bush. Though LZ Ross was fairly close to where I'd been fighting before, the countryside looked quite different. It was green and overgrown with trees and vegetation, primarily because there had been very little bombing in the area in deference to the civilian population. Occasionally you saw bomb craters, but they were a rarity; and there were no cleared-out areas like Leatherneck Square. All of the rich growth made for a slightly more picturesque landscape and a considerably more dangerous one, since the number of hiding places increased significantly in these settled areas.

I went out for my first killer team mission with Sergeant Meyer, a dark-skinned man with a brush mustache who was all business; Corporal Moore, a big blond kid from Boston, whom we nicknamed the "Boston Fly," or simply "Fly"; Sam Green—short, black, from Cleveland; and one other guy whose name I've forgotten.

The reason I've forgotten is that he wasn't around very long. We were winding down a dark road sometime after midnight when suddenly a shot rang out and this guy ahead of me fell like a sack of meal. I thought he was dead until I bent over him, and saw that his eyes were still in focus and that he was conscious. Then I looked down at his chest and knew he wouldn't be around too long.

"Call a medevac chopper," I told Meyer as he crawled back to where we were. "He's hit and needs attention quick."

Meyer got on the radio while I tried to make the poor guy comfortable while he waited for the end, which I knew wouldn't be too long.

Then I noticed he was trying to say something, and I bent over.

"Shotgun," he whispered. "Keep shotgun."

I looked around and saw the gleaming barrel lying in the tall grass. Not a long barrel. It had been sawed off to about 12 inches. Then I understood. Private weaponry was against regulations, and he didn't want the gun put on the helicopter with him.

"I'll keep it and bring it back with me. You can get it when you're out of the hospital."

He nodded and seemed relieved, but his eyes were beginning to glaze; and I knew he needn't worry about being court-martialed for possession of the shotgun.

When the helicopter arrived about a half hour later he was already unconscious, and later, when we got back in, we found out that he'd died before they even landed back at the base.

So I had a shotgun from the first night I went out on a killer team. Its advantages as a weapon are obvious to anyone who has hunted. For close combat you couldn't beat it, since all you had to do was fire in the direction of the enemy rather than make a precise hit with a rifle bullet. And a sawed-off shotgun could turn a head into 20 pounds of hamburger with just a squeeze of the trigger. All in all I felt a little more comfortable with it. A lot of guys had them and the officers didn't look too carefully, particularly the veterans in Vietnam, since they knew the fighting conditions.

After the sniper fire we knew the Cong were out that night, though we didn't know how many or what they were up to. So after the chopper had picked up the wounded man, we moved carefully into a nearby settlement, hoping to flush out the sniper and whoever was with him.

The peasants lived in little hooches made of grass and wood that stood no more than six feet high and were as primitive as anything in Africa or the South Sea Islands. They kept most of the rain off and provided some shelter against the wind—but that was about all. Certainly they didn't keep people like us out, which was both a blessing and a curse as far as we were concerned, since many a Marine stepped into one of those rickety hooches and either went up in sudden flame or else had his throat slit.

As we entered the small settlement, Meyer indicated that he and Green would take the second hooch and Moore and I should take the first. I signaled to Moore to cover me and stepped inside. On the floor I saw a young woman lying down, holding a baby in her arms. It was a typical domestic scene, with one exception: Where was the man?

Moore followed me in and began questioning her in what sounded like Vietnamese to me, though it was undoubtedly some bastard form. She told him that her husband was not around anymore, that the Vietcong had come and taken him away. It was the standard story they all told, but often enough it was true.

So we left her alone and rejoined Meyer and Green, who'd had no better luck. Then we moved out of the settlement, with me walking point, every muscle straining, eyes alert. Already I was carrying the shotgun rather than the M-16, and I felt considerably safer. If one of them popped up in front of me, I wouldn't have to aim too carefully.

The Vietcong had covered the entire area with bunkers they used as contingency hiding places. They'd been digging them for years in the sides of mountains and hills; and some hills were honeycombed to the point that there was no way we could destroy or even patrol them all. As we moved up the slope just outside the settlement, I glanced over and saw a dark man-sized hole with an overhang you could walk over. I glanced at it for a moment, then started to move on. But for an instant the dark eye glowed red, then quickly faded. Somebody had lit a fire inside. That was where our sniper was hiding.

Remembering he'd already killed one of us, I moved as quietly and as cautiously forward as I could, with Moore right behind. I was trying to figure out the best way to take him. I needed to put some light on him in order to get a clear shot. I was carrying a pistol as well as a flashlight, and for an instant I considered the possibility of going in like Sam Spade, flashlight in the left hand, pistol in the right.

But I rejected that approach, because I knew that if he had a rifle I'd be at a disadvantage. I'd have to get too close to have a sure shot. So I decided to try out the shotgun. It had brought the other guy bad luck. Maybe it would do better for me.

I waited until Moore slipped up beside me and then whispered, "I'm going to illuminate the inside of that cave with a grenade. Then I'm going in fast with my shotgun. If the gook hits me, you take him out with your rifle."

Moore nodded uncertainly, and in the darkness I couldn't see enough of his face to tell whether or not he was afraid. I had enough things to worry about without my backup being shaky. Slowly, quietly I inched toward the mouth of the hole, figuring I'd get as close as I could, because I had only one try for him before he got me. When I was no more than eight feet

away, he was suddenly framed in the round O of
the cave. We saw each other simultaneously. His
rifle jerked up, and I began to blast away, pump-
ing shotgun rounds into the darkness. As I did, I
was aware of tracer rounds whizzing past my
knees, and I vaguely knew that Moore was
sprawled beside me, firing his M-16 on auto-
matic. No problem with my backup.

When we stopped firing we heard nothing
but silence. We waited a full minute, not moving
a muscle. Then I decided to toss a hand grenade
into the cave and see if the blast would finish off
anything that was left. So I pulled the pin,
heaved in the grenade, then leaped on top of the
cave mouth, expecting to feel the earth shake
and roar underneath me.

Nothing happened.

I eased back over to where Moore was
standing.

"It must have been a dud," I whispered.

"Did you remove the safety latch?"

I looked at him in disbelief.

"What do you mean, 'safety latch'?"

I couldn't believe what I was hearing.

"All the grenades have them now," he said.
"I'm surprised you weren't told."

Then he showed me how to remove the
safety latch.

So armed with a second hand grenade I
moved back toward the cave, this time with the
safety latch removed. Again I tossed the grenade
and jumped up on the bunker top. This time
both grenades went off and I collapsed into the
mouth of the cave, afraid for a second I was going to be buried alive.

Moore helped me up and we stared at what

remained of the bunker. Somewhere underneath the mound of dirt and rock was a dead
Cong, that much we knew; but we didn't bother
to dig him out. We figured we might as well let
him sleep in his brand new grave. At least he
wouldn't be picking off any more Marines.

Moving on up the hill we passed a huge rock, 50
to 60 feet wide and about 30 feet high. As we
followed the path that led by the rock, I noticed
that a smaller trail wound off and seemed to go
right into the rock, so I followed it. Sure enough,
instead of just stopping there, the trail dipped
into a hollow cave just under the rock. Moore
and I moved in very carefully, figuring it was
probably a Cong hideout.

What we found was a meeting room of
some sort, with chairs and a table. We figured
this was a place where they planned strategy
and initiated their operations. With something
this elaborate and permanent, they had to have
a fairly large bunch active in this area. So we left
more cautiously than we'd entered, a couple of
Goldilockses who were happy the bears had
been out.

We rejoined Meyer and Green; and farther
up the hill we saw two hooches, enough to call
the place a village, I suppose. It was reasonable
to assume that some of these people were involved in the operation carried on from under
the rock, though it was something you usually
couldn't prove. All you could do was question
them and if they looked suspicious, haul them
back to LZ Ross and let the experts have a go at
them.

Green and I slipped into the first hooch and

saw a guy curled up on the floor, clutching something in his hands like a security blanket. I bent forward to look and saw it was a North Vietnamese parachute, so this was probably a regular, somebody who'd been dropped in for a particular operation.

I eased the shotgun down and suddenly jammed it against his nose. His eyes flipped open and then widened with fear, but he didn't utter a sound. He was well-trained. We took him outside and Green guarded him while I went back to check another room. Sure enough there was another one.

I hauled him outside just in time to hear shouts from the other hooch and to see two or three shadow-figures rush out and disappear into the darkness. Had they killed Meyer and Moore and then run?

We didn't have long to wait for an answer, because the two of them came out of the hooch with two prisoners of their own. Now there were four of us against four of them, though the guns did make a big difference. Obviously we were finished for the evening. We'd have to get the prisoners down the hill without getting bushwhacked, not an easy assignment under the circumstances, particularly with their buddies out there in the night, probably with weapons.

We searched the hooches and came up with some rope and the parachute, so we gagged all four, blindfolded them, and then tied them together—the rope around their necks so they would be even less tempted to try an escape.

We worked our way down cautiously, trying to avoid the trails, moving through brush and between trees. I led the way, rope in hand, seldom glancing back. Then I felt a jerk on the line. I jerked back, giving the prisoners the message that they weren't to hold us up. The rope jerked again, this time harder, so I gave it a real wrench and heard a gurgling sound.

I stopped to see what the hell was going on, and Moore, who was bringing up the rear, seemed puzzled as well. We finally figured out that he had been responsible for the first jerk when he stumbled. I'd jerked back, and we'd gotten into a tug o' war—harmless enough to us, but more than uncomfortable for the four whose necks were in nooses. Their eyes were popping out of their heads. I started to feel sorry for them, then changed my mind. If they had the opportunity, they'd slice my head off without the slightest twinge of conscience.

It took us from 0300 hours until daylight to get in with our catch—a distance of not more than a click, but all eight of us got there alive. When we'd turned the prisoners over to the company command post I was excited.

"Where you going on your R-and-R?" I asked Moore.

"What R-and-R?"

"The three days you get for bringing in prisoners."

He laughed.

"Nobody gets a reward around here for bringing in prisoners. We got all the prisoners we can handle at LZ Ross."

"What do they do with them?" I asked.

"Get all the information they can—which usually isn't much. They hold them for a few months. Then they 'repatriate' them."

I told him I hoped that didn't mean what I thought it meant.

"That's right," he said. "They go right back, dig up their weapons, and they're at it again. There are guys who've actually captured the same gook twice."

Late the next morning I stopped by and asked my company commander, Lieutenant Ambort, what he'd found out from questioning the prisoners.

"Not a whole bunch about what they were up to," he said, "except we determined that one is a VC, one is a North Vietnamese regular and a sergeant, one is a Chinese Communist adviser, and one is a paymaster."

"Isn't that a strange mixture?" I asked.

Lieutenant Ambort shrugged his shoulders.

"They may be up to something."

We found out what it was soon enough.

It was an attack by sappers.

You didn't hear much about sappers in the American TV reports of the Vietnam War. As a matter of fact, most people I know who followed the war closely have told me they never heard the word, much less knew such people existed. But sappers were responsible for a lot of U.S. casualties in that war.

Sappers were suicide attackers, a lot like the kamikaze pilots in World War II. They went into missions knowing they would be killed, perfectly willing to die. When an enemy doesn't care whether or not he survives, he poses special problems and can accomplish important objectives.

The sappers would have all their blood circulation tied off at the joints by rope tourniquets so that if their arms or legs were blown off, they could still keep coming without bleeding to death immediately. Sometimes a sapper would have a satchel of explosives strapped around his chest with a hand grenade to detonate the whole business. Then he would find a group of Marines, plunge into the middle of them, and pull the pin.

I heard that sappers were always pumped so full of opium that they were in a near frenzy, but the opium may have been used to deaden the pain rather than to induce a wild, self-destructive state, so they could carry out their mission, even though one arm was gone.

The communist use of sappers was another reason why our orders not to fire unless fired upon were at times difficult or impossible to follow. If a sapper came running across an open field, loaded down with explosives, ready to blow up an entire company, you would have to be certain of what he had inside the satchel before you blew him away—assuming it wasn't too late.

Not all sappers wasted themselves the first time out. Some of them continued to run extremely dangerous missions until finally they were killed or captured. Certainly they were among the most effective behind-the-lines fighters that the communists had, and I am still curious as to how they got them to run these suicide missions.

Of course war does deaden your sensibilities, though usually not to the point where you are willing to go out and take risks that are beyond reason. As I look back on the way we were in 1969, I realize the degree to which the day-to-day business of killing people hardened us to the act. It had to, otherwise we wouldn't have been any good at it. You can't kill the enemy effectively if you grieve over each victim, wondering about his wife or children, thinking about the many ramifications of taking a human life. Those are questions you answer before you go into the service, then try to forget on the front lines.

Our best way of forgetting was to treat combat as lightly as we could, to make a game of it. So when I started out on the killer teams, I found that there was keen competition between platoons and companies as to how many they killed and in what exotic ways the job was done. It was grisly sport, and sometimes it led to real dangers.

The next night two kill teams were sent out, so naturally the stakes were upped in the game we were playing, and each team wanted to outshine the other. We had a new member of our team, a guy who had a lot of time in-country and had been out on plenty of missions. He had decided to show up the other team by killing one of the enemy with a bowie knife, just so he could say he'd done it. With this purpose in mind, he'd gotten hold of one of the knives and that night was carrying it for the first time, desperate to try it out, hoping to run into some action.

We went back up the same hill, even more cautious than before. They'd be on guard for us this time. The new guy had his bowie knife in his right hand and his M-16 in his left, daring anyone to leap out of the brush and attack him; but he seemed doomed to disappointment. We didn't run into any Vietcong until we hit a small village and began entering the hooches. That's when he got to use his knife.

We came to a cluster of hooches, and we told him that his time had come. If there was an armed Vietcong in there, he could cut his head off. Of course, we were joking. It never occurred to us that he'd actually enter a hooch without his rifle. But he did! He rushed right in before anyone had time to change his mind or tell him it was a joke.

When he charged into the room, he got just what he'd been praying for—a regular North Vietnamese soldier, asleep, cradling his rifle. The presence of the rifle was all he needed. With a yell he leaped forward and began flailing at the soldier, expecting arms and ears to be flying off in all directions.

But either the knife was dull or the Vietnamese soldier was especially thick-skinned; because the knife barely broke the skin. With a cry the Vietnamese grabbed his weapon, aimed it, and was about to blow the kid away, when two of us fired at the same time and dropped him in his tracks. Then we told the kid to throw his bowie knife away and fight the way the Marines had taught him to fight. Reluctantly he agreed, but that wasn't the end of that kind of grim competition.

When we got back, our team was told we'd be off for a couple of days; so Moore and I decided to hunt up some whisky and do some serious partying—and we knew where to go. No one below the rank of staff sergeant was allowed to buy whisky in Vietnam, but over in the staff ser-

geants' hooch there was always plenty of the
stuff, if you had the money. So that night we
dropped in to pay our respects to a couple of
staff sergeants we knew.

We had killed almost a fifth between us
when the sappers hit. We heard the shouts, the
explosions, and the sound of running. Then
there was gunfire from every direction. We
knew in an instant that we'd been hit and overrun, and this was more or less confirmed when
the roof above us was blown off by a mortar
shell.

Moore was first outside and I was right on
his heels. We could see people running in every
direction and here and there Marines were firing back.

"2nd Platoon on the road!" somebody
shouted, and we recognized Lieutenant Lewis.

The knowledge of what was happening
sobered us up a little, but not nearly enough. We
stumbled back to our hooch and discovered that
the lights were out, so we had to search around
for our gear in the dark while we were half-
drunk. I finally put my hand on my shotgun,
found my "boony cap" with the slots for ammunition, and also put on my M-79 grenade vest,
which held ten grenades. All Moore managed to
locate was his rifle, but that was enough for him.

"Let's go gook hunting," he yelled, and we
staggered out into the night. We made our way
toward the outer perimeter, and the first thing
we saw was a staff sergeant lying on the ground,
wounded in the leg.

"Get back," he yelled. "There's a gook behind that rock."

We weren't about to "get back." This was exactly the kind of situation we were looking for. To our right was the rock, where the Vietcong was supposed to be hiding. Behind the rock was a privy, where he might also be. The sergeant was lying on the ground in our path. And beyond him we saw another Marine, crouching behind a sandbag. He couldn't move without walking in front of the rock.

Moore turned to me with a drunken grin.

"I'm going to diddy bop over to that sandbag, and when the gook sticks his head out from behind the rock or out of the outhouse, you blow it off. Okay?"

It sounded great to me, so I drew a bead between the rock and the outhouse, while Moore went sailing across the open space and slid in behind the sandbag. The Marine already there looked at Moore as if he were crazy.

No response from behind the rock.

So Moore came back, this time at a slow amble, his legs still a little rubbery.

No response.

At that point Moore started laughing at the guy crouching behind the sandbag.

"Come on out, chickenshit, there's nothing behind that rock."

A little ashamed of himself now, the guy stood up, grinned, and walked out into the open.

At that moment a torso appeared from behind the rock and started to blast away at the poor guy, as if he had a grudge against him and him alone. The guy managed to get back behind the sandbag again, but he was shaken.

Moore scratched his head.

"Herrod," he said, "what can we do?"

I studied the situation for a moment or two, trying to think straight.

"Let's frag him."

I handed Moore a grenade, took one myself, and when I nodded, we both tossed our grenades between the rock and the outhouse. One grenade got the Vietcong and the other got the outhouse, and brown rain poured down on us for several seconds.

After everything had settled, Moore went over to what was left of the sapper and let out a cry.

"He's got one of those Red Star buckles on him, and I want it."

Red Star buckles were rare, and you were considered lucky if you picked one up.

"Be careful," I yelled to Moore. "He may be booby trapped."

"No way," said Moore, bending over the shapeless remains.

"A sapper?" I reminded him.

Moore stood up, still swaying a little.

"You're right. I better be careful."

So he undid the buckle very slowly while I stood at a distance, wondering if he was sober enough to get the buckle off. Suddenly he lost patience, jerked the whole belt off, hoisting the body two feet in the air, and then ran. If the body had been booby trapped, you wouldn't have been able to separate what was left of him from what was left of the sapper. But he was lucky—and he had his buckle.

About that time Lieutenant Lewis spotted us and yelled over.

"Herrod and Moore. You two come along

with us. We got to plug up the hole where those sappers broke through."

"What the hell happened?" I asked as we moved out beyond the perimeter.

"They slipped up on those Seabees who were standing line," Lieutenant Lewis said. "Killed twenty of them and broke through."

"How did they do it?"

"Slit their throats."

If I hadn't drunk so much that would have sobered me up, but it was still pretty much of a lark to me.

We moved quietly through the darkness until we reached a ditch about three feet deep.

"This is the trench," said Lieutenant Lewis. "It runs right on out into that field. There are probably gooks at the other end. We need to move down about a hundred feet, then stop."

Suddenly we heard the whistle of a mortar, followed almost immediately by a flash and a loud *kabloom*. I hit the ditch first, and Moore and a BNG named Bob Butler jumped in behind me. Then the others followed. There were about 30 of us in all. But Lieutenant Lewis didn't quite make it, and I saw him lying on the edge of the ditch, holding his leg and swearing. It was too dark to tell how badly he was hit, but someone was with him and we had our orders.

"Let's go," I said.

This was Butler's first time out. He was short, blond, and I could see in his eyes that he was scared.

"Well, Butler," I said, "it's about time you started earning your money."

He grinned, and I knew he would be all right.

With Moore and me on either side of him, he must have figured that he was in good company, so the three of us strolled along as if we hadn't a care in the world, while I was laughing at the thought of that outhouse flying in a million pieces. Something to write home about. People knew about outhouses in Oklahoma.

Then I suddenly stopped. Lieutenant Lewis had said something about a hundred feet.

"Anybody behind us?" I whispered back to Moore.

He looked.

"Not a soul."

"Oh, God," I said.

"What's wrong?" Butler asked, catching something in my voice.

"We're out beyond our own lines," I whispered. "We're somewhere in the middle."

"So what does that mean?"

"It means," said Moore, "that we can't move in either direction. At each end of this ditch is somebody who will blast our butts the moment they see us."

"So what can we do?" Butler asked.

"I don't know about you," I said. "But I'm going to sleep."

I slid down in the cold, muddy ditch.

"Good idea," Moore said, and slid down, too.

The next thing I knew it was morning, and I opened my eyes to see Butler sitting there, arms wrapped around his waist, as he peered in first one direction and then the other.

One good thing came out of the sapper breakthrough—we didn't have to go out on sweeps

with the ARVNs the next day. ARVN stood for
the Army of the Republic of Viet Nam, and they
were supposed to be fighting on our side. But
you never really knew. Sometimes we had an
idea that the entire crew was a communist plot,
and at other times we thought they were just
cowardly and incompetent.

It was a funny war, unlike any Americans
had ever fought before. We didn't fraternize with
our ARVN allies and had almost nothing to do
with the villagers who surrounded us on all
sides, watching us move among them to kill the
Vietcong in their midst. In World War II, even
the occupation army soon became friendly with
its former enemies, but we never got to know
our friends in Vietnam, the people for whom we
were risking our lives.

On our way back to camp that morning,
something happened that perhaps best typifies
the American experience in Vietnam. Walking
along the path, we met a group of children going
out into the fields. Ordinarily kids in any country are friendly with the military; but as we ap-
proached them, they quickly veered over to one
side of the path like a covey of quail. All the
while they kept their eyes down, leaning away
from us as they scurried past. No one said a
word.

Just as we turned the bend, I glanced back
and caught a couple of the children looking at us
over their shoulders, and I waved. They turned
their heads quickly and were gone around a
curve. Not running, just walking at the same
plodding pace.

I don't know what these children thought
about us. If their parents were Vietcong, then

they hated us, having been filled with all kinds of propaganda about the cruelty and greed of Americans. But if they were the children of ordinary parents, they wouldn't have thought too much better of us, if only because wherever we went we brought trouble—and usually death.

I think people like that never understand or care about politics, even today when the communists are filling their heads with all sorts of slogans and chants and marching them up and down streets. The country people in Oklahoma are the same way, at least most of them. They may vote, and sometimes they'll even watch a speech on television. But most of the time they're interested in other, more immediate things, figuring that whoever is elected won't be that much better or worse than the other fellow.

I'm not sure that's the best way to be, given the importance of politics in our age. But I think people live longer and are more contented if they don't worry about things they can't change. And that was surely true of the Vietnamese peasants, who were (and continue to be) the greatest victims of what has happened in that part of the world. Though I seldom think about the Vietnam people as a whole, occasionally I wonder what happened to those children after they went around the bend.

We got back just in time to see Lieutenant Lewis being medevacked out.

"How is he?" I shouted to one of the corpsmen, standing near the chopper, his hair blowing in the rush of air from the blades.

"Shot in the hip," he yelled back. "He'll be okay."

I watched as the corpsman climbed in and

they roared off. So I had lost my second platoon leader. I would see him again on my way back to the States, recovered and pulling easy duty; but I hated to see him go. He was a good Marine and knew what he was doing in the field. He understood the risks; and when they were too high, he didn't take them.

However, like Lieutenant North, he also knew why we were over there; and he could give the best inspirational talks I ever heard, always ending up by shouting like a preacher, "And now men we will go out and do battle with the hated Cong!" We thought it was funny—and he intended it to be—but he fired us up all the same.

His replacement, Lieutenant Carney, was another matter. A good man who had learned his theory well, he'd had little or no experience in combat when he took over; and for a while it was pretty hairy for everybody. We went out on sweeps and killer team missions with him for several weeks, but he was always hesitant and confused when we ran into trouble.

Some people naturally take to warfare and some don't. While I was scared about half the time I moved into the field, I discovered that I enjoyed hunting and killing the enemy, and I did it well. Bob Butler was a natural too. Within two or three weeks he was as calm as anyone out there, and the other guys began to look up to him almost immediately. Lieutenant Carney, on the other hand, was a slow learner, in part because he had to worry about the duties of command in addition to his own rear end, in part because he had no love of the hunt, no imagination, and therefore no aptitude for anticipating inevitabilities.

I found this out one day when we were on a sweep through a series of rice paddies. A rice paddy is something out of a bad dream, the ground you try to run on when you can't move and something is about to get you. Rice paddies are a foot deep in water, and it takes you forever to cross them, particularly when you are hauling an M-60 machine gun. So that day, when we came to yet another paddy, we were hoping Lieutenant Carney would take the long way around, or else back off until we got some help. For two straight days sweep teams had tried to make that crossing and had been mowed down by a 50-caliber machine gun hidden somewhere in the middle of the waving green rice. Surely, we thought, the lieutenant would know better than to send us out across this particular rice paddy.

I watched him as he scanned the middle of the field, looking for the 50-caliber machine gun; and I wanted to tell him that we wouldn't see it till it opened fire, and it wouldn't do that until the platoon was in the middle of the paddy, ankle deep in mud. But I kept my mouth shut, hoping he would figure it out for himself.

No such luck! He turned to the 40 men standing behind him, their teeth clenched, and in a matter-of-fact voice said, "Okay, men. We're going across. The machine gun teams will cover for us."

Then he turned to me.

"Herrod," he said, "you'll set up the two machine gun teams over there on that high ground.

That way you'll be able to see the 50-caliber if it opens fire."

In the first place, the rise he was pointing to wasn't the "high ground" they talk about in the strategy books. It was a small lump in the earth, about the elevation of a good manure pile. Just high enough to put you on a pedestal so you'd be easy to knock off.

"Sir," I said, "you can't face a 50-caliber machine gun with nothing but an M-60."

"Two M-60s," he said.

"With *ten* M-60s, particularly stuck up on that mound."

"There's no other way," he said.

I tried to explain to him that there was always another way when you were contemplating sure death, but he was determined.

"I need you to protect the rest of the platoon."

I looked in his eyes and could tell that he wasn't going to change his mind. For a moment I hated him, then it occurred to me that he was too green to know what he was asking. A cold numbness began to settle over me.

"Okay," I said. "But I don't want the full teams. Just two of us."

"Why?" he asked.

"Because whoever is firing those machine guns when that 50-caliber opens up is going to be ripped to shreds in a matter of seconds, whether it's two of us or eight."

"Okay," he said. "Who do you want?"

It was a hard choice for a couple of reasons. Under ordinary circumstances you wouldn't want to show preference for one of your team members over another. Everyone would know that with your life on the line, you would pick the man you had the most respect for—and that would say something about the others.

In this case, however, it would be a dubious honor, since in all likelihood the guy you chose would be dead beside you in a matter of seconds. So maybe the others wouldn't be so disappointed after all.

I pretended to be thinking, but I'd already made up my mind.

"I'll take Butler," I said.

Though he'd only been in-country for about a month, he still had been there longer than most of the others. Besides, I knew he wasn't afraid to die.

Sure enough, he moved out of line with no hesitation, hauling one of the M-60s, as Moore handed me the other. They looked like a couple of playtoys compared to the 50-caliber hidden somewhere in the field.

"You don't have to do this," I told Butler as we walked over to what Lieutenant Carney was calling the "high ground."

"It's okay," he said.

"No, its *not* okay," I said. "That stupid son of a bitch is going to get us killed. There's no way these two popguns are going to take out a 50-caliber machine gun, unless we happen to hit him the first five seconds after he starts firing. If we don't do that, you can bend down and kiss your ass goodbye."

"Okay," he said, "what do we do?"

"First, we line up all the ammunition and link it together. We've got twenty-four cans. We'll divide them—twelve apiece."

Lieutenant Carney was over talking to the

rest of the platoon, giving out assignments; so I took out a piece of C-4, lit it, and cooked myself a Last Supper. Moore and some of the others came over and talked for a while. They knew why I was eating the meal, and they thought I was probably right.

"Herrod, you guys ready?" Lieutenant Carney called.

I nodded and lay down behind one of the guns, while Butler lay down behind the other.

"Our best bet is for me to aim high and you to aim low. Then we'll try to come together right on him. We got maybe three seconds before he spots us and swings the gun around."

Three to seven seconds. I remembered.

We watched as the first group of four or five slipped into the rice paddy and began to slosh across. They tried to be as quiet as possible, but they sounded like a herd of hippopotamuses. I kept my eyes on the center of the paddy, waiting for the first gleam, listening for the first click, not expecting to hear it until the platoon was strung out across the rice paddy like a human rope.

Neither Butler nor I said a word, and we breathed as quietly as possible. Then, when the whole bunch was exposed, I whispered, "Now."

But nothing happened. They'd apparently pulled out the machine gun the previous night, figuring after two tries to make it across, no American officer would be stupid enough to do it again. But Lieutenant Carney had fooled them!

It's difficult for anyone who wasn't there—even World War II and Korean veterans—to understand how it felt to live and fight out of a fenced-in corral right in the middle of your enemy's country. It did you little good to stay back at the fire base, because the Vietcong didn't always wait for you to come looking for them. Often they came looking for you. So any stroll outside the bunker could be your last.

One day on my way back from chow, I stopped in the heat of the sun to talk to Lieutenant Ambort.

"Herrod," he said, "we need to . . ."

Suddenly a round tore through his flak jacket, missing his neck by less than a half inch. We both hit the ground, maneuvering to use our weapons. I was packing two .45s at the moment, so I pulled out one and began firing at a green tree just outside the perimeter. Soon everyone else was blasting away too, just like pioneers shooting out of a wagon circle at invisible Indians. It was the same old game. They got off one round, and we responded with ten thousand. But their one shot was sometimes right on target, and to my knowledge we never hit anything.

I had fifty rounds of ammunition on me at the time, so I lay there, firing at the tree, knowing for certain that no one was hiding there. And I didn't stop until I'd fired off the last round. The futility of it struck me at the time, and I laughed at myself. But the longer I thought about it, the less funny it seemed. I suppose more than any incident during my tour of duty, it struck closest to the heart of why we would never beat these people.

Whether in the north fighting the regulars or in the south fighting the Cong, we were always in a cage of our own making, being fired at by enemies who had free run of the country and would shoot at us from outside the cage, then turn into trees while we assaulted the wilderness.

By then I was going into the field with ten hand grenades, two .45s in my belt, a shotgun, and an M-16 rifle. Each of these weapons had a different use, and at one time or another I killed the enemy with all of them.

I would never have carried all this hardware around with me in the 3rd Marines, not with Lieutenant North in command. There we were fighting regulars with conventional tactics and conventional weapons—and doing fairly well. Down at LZ Ross, we were fighting guerrillas and terrorists, and almost anything went on our side too. The philosophy among those who fought in the Ashaw Valley was simple: Let's do to them what they're doing to us.

I had proven myself on a number of occasions since I came down from the north, and they all knew about the Silver Star; so they left me alone in the field, letting me do my own thing. Even Lieutenant Carney, after he'd been there a while, seldom gave me any orders, and never gave me any advice. He knew I had been around long enough to do the right thing without being told. And there were even times when I refused to do what he said. So I was fighting in a different Marine Corps from the one in which Lieutenant Oliver North had served.

The night after the sniper fire, Moore and I took a killer team out, and when we came back in the next morning, Lieutenant Carney told us we could stand lines for the rest of the day and then sleep that night. Standing lines in the daytime was good duty, because you could put one guy in the hole at a time and the rest could sleep. Our platoon had only one segment of the perimeter to cover, and there were three or four killer teams sharing the duty. I figured I could sleep for six hours at the least before somebody woke me up.

As I prepared to slide under the hooch tent, I saw the rest of the 2nd Platoon march out. I grinned, put my helmet under my head, and closed my eyes. The next day and night would be the nearest thing I knew to a weekend.

For some reason or other I didn't go right to sleep, so when all hell broke loose I heard the racket. The shots and explosions sounded as if they were 600 or 700 yards away. Just about where the 2nd Platoon should have been. We all knew what had happened. They had run into an ambush.

Lieutenant Ambort came running over.

"You guys that just came in, stand lines! I'm going to round up the rest of the company."

He didn't know us very well.

"Hell, no!" I yelled. "We'll go! We'll go!"

"We'll walk point," Moore chimed in, grabbing up his gear.

And Butler and the others were running back and forth, snatching at rifles and hand grenades, dancing around, excited at the prospect of a firefight. We'd had a dull night. Now we'd see action for sure.

Lieutenant Ambort didn't seem to notice that we'd disobeyed his order. It didn't even occur to us that we were doing it. If Lieutenant North had told me to stand lines, I would have done it. But then I don't think he would have tried to leave us behind when our own platoon was in trouble.

We took out across the field at a gallop, with Lieutenant Ambort behind us. When we got there, we immediately saw what had happened: They had been caught in an ambush trying to cross a rice paddy. They were pinned down by machine gun fire.

A sergeant from another platoon came sloshing across the paddy, and from somewhere in the brush across the way a machine gun fired a burst and we could see the tracers flash through the reeds and tear into the water. But they hit short of the sergeant, and he made it.

"We got men scattered along the far side," he gasped. "And out there in the paddy, sir, we got nine men dead."

"Nine?" Lieutenant Ambort said.

"I believe it's nine, sir. They haven't moved or made a sound. You can see one of them straight through there."

He pointed, and I saw the guy. He was floating facedown in the water, looking as dead as any human being could.

Lieutenant Ambort turned and looked at me, then at Moore.

"Herrod," he said, "I need your gun set up on the other side of the rice paddy—to cover."

"That's crazy!" Butler burst out. "Everybody's already been shot."

"I need that gun over there," Ambort said evenly.

Butler glanced over at me, expecting me to volunteer to carry the gun.

"Don't look at me," I said. "It's your turn in the barrel."

So Butler got up, ready to make the run. So did Green and I. Then Ambort turned to me.

"After we make it across, I want you to help me get those bodies out of this paddy so we can haul them back."

We stood there and watched while Butler took the machine gun, braced himself, and then started sloshing out across the rice paddy, the water up to his knees. The 50-caliber barked from across the paddy, and Butler took a dive to safety. Then Green followed with the ammo. He made it too. Then I came barreling through the water, hauling my shotgun, rifle, ammo, grenades, and two pistols. I'd weighed a couple of days earlier in full pack and found I was over three hundred pounds—about 220 of which was me. But I made it.

Then from behind I heard a voice. It was Moore.

"Herrod!" he called. "I'm coming out too."

But he didn't make it. A single shot rang out, probably from a sniper in a tree, and Moore fell like a log somewhere in the reeds. I yelled, but there was no answer. Then the 50-caliber began to rake the grass again, and from all over, our platoon answered with shots.

Lieutenant Carney joined us, and we started out into the tall grass to find the bodies. We half-waded, half-swam while we heard bursts of fire and the spitting of the rounds as they tore into the water.

And one by one we found them: a corpsman, with his chest torn half away; another with a hole in him so small we could hardly find it;

two guys I didn't know, and the last, one I did know—Sergeant Lyons. I remembered him as a talkative guy with a beer in his hand. He had been hit in the face; and while there was a neat hole just above his eye, the back of his head was a bloody crater. When I hoisted his water-soaked body over my shoulder, I made little connection between it and the man I knew.

I hauled the last one back, and looked around, expecting to see Moore there as well. But no one had pulled him out yet. I turned to go back. Then I saw him, leaning up against a tree, bloody bandages on both sides of his face.

Butler was with him, and he looked up as I came over.

"He took one through both cheeks. Didn't touch his jaw or his teeth."

I started laughing.

"So they couldn't get you!"

Moore frowned at me.

"What does that mean?" Butler asked. "What are you talking about?"

"Moore has been going around saying that the gooks could never put a bullet in him because he's too fast and too smart."

I laughed at him again. He looked miserable.

"What's the matter? Can't you talk?" I asked.

He reached in his pocket, pulled out a pencil and pad, and scribbled something, tore off the sheet, and handed it to me.

It read: "FUCK YOU, HERROD."

By this time the battalion had moved forward in full force, choppers and gun ships were sweeping the area, and the Vietcong had disappeared back into their holes. While everyone was evacuating, Butler and I were covering for them, watching for the only real danger, which was snipers.

We weren't paying any attention to the choppers overhead because we knew they were all ours. Then something happened that made us a little more careful, even about our own guys. A gun ship swept in low and fired a phosphorus marking rocket. Standing on the paddy dike, we watched with growing disbelief as the rocket veered and headed straight for us, trailing billows of white smoke. When it exploded about fifteen feet away it knocked us both into the air and we landed facedown in the rice paddy. For an instant I thought I was dead. Then I jumped up and ran for one of the choppers, with Butler right behind me. Our feet never touched the water as we watched the gun ship make a turn at the far end of the paddy and start back.

The next day they decided enough was enough. That particular area had cost too many lives and too much time. So they swept the landscape with the entire battalion, trying to find out where the armament was stashed, where the troops were hiding. After a couple of days they found what they were looking for—a whole mountain dug out like a honeycomb, an underground city complete with sleeping rooms, storage areas, and a hospital. But this time the enemy had gotten too greedy for blood and had killed too many of our men; so we blew it all up, collapsing a mountain on all who were hiding. We may have killed three hundred and we may have killed thousands, we neither knew nor cared. Nor, I suspect, did the North Vietnamese and their bosses, the Chinese.

BAD TROUBLE

WHEN WE CAME back to the command post that afternoon, Lieutenant Ambort called me into the duty hut, something he rarely did. He was only three years older than I was, and the kind of officer who let his men alone as long as they seemed to be doing their jobs—and I was doing mine. I was by then the most experienced man in the platoon, and though I had lost my stripes, everyone continued to call me "corporal," even in official military proceedings. I began to notice that the younger guys, the ones who had been in-country only a few weeks, were hanging around me a lot, asking me questions, getting me to tell war stories. I wasn't Rambo, but I was one of the best Marines on the base. So when Ambort called me in, I wasn't worried, but I was curious.

"Herrod," he said, "you got any clean utilities?"

"I've got some fairly clean ones," I said.

"Well, I guess they'll have to do," he said, "because the day after tomorrow you're going to be awarded the Silver Star by the battalion commander. *Stars and Stripes* will be here to take your picture. You'll be famous."

I nodded and said I'd be happy to get the medal.

It seemed like years since Lieutenant North had sent in the recommendation; and while I had expected to receive the decoration eventually, I'd put it out of my mind. For a second I wondered where Blue and Ernie were. They were the two guys who should have been there for the ceremony, since they most understood what it was all about.

But the fact I was being awarded the Silver Star didn't get me out of any tough duty. The next day in the field three of our platoon members were killed by booby traps, and another bunch was caught in an ambush. Six were killed. All of the action centered in Sector 4 of the Queson Valley, near a village called Son Trang 4, where a band of Vietcong and their sympathizers were killing off Marines almost daily.

Lieutenant Ambort, who was easygoing most of the time, was shaken by these losses. We were being torn to pieces by a bunch of hard-core peasant guerrillas whose activities were being directed by communist organizers in the district. First Sergeant Lyons and four other men had been killed. Now these latest casualties. So Ambort had blood in his eye, when he heard about it, and he came out to where I was standing lines to give me orders.

"Herrod, I want you to lead a patrol into Sector 4. Make this one special. We'll call it Big Lyons 4, in memory of Sarge. We're going to pay the little bastards back, you understand?"

I told him that I understood perfectly. We were all ready to get our pound of flesh.

"If you see anybody," he said, "shoot first, ask questions later."

I nodded. Nothing new about that advice. As I turned to leave, he called after me. "Get me some tonight!"

I nodded and went to get my team together.

This time it consisted of Mike Schwartz, Sam Green, and two guys I didn't know too well named Tom Boyd and Mike Krichten. I would be the team leader, and Schwartz, with time in-country and proven guts, would be point man. I told them we'd be trying to hit the Cong in retaliation for what had happened to our own men, and I repeated some of the things the lieutenant had said. Everyone understood, of course, that while feelings were running high, we would still be in the same old fight with the same old enemy. After all, basic tactics don't really change and high feelings can sometimes get you into trouble.

Near sundown I ate my Last Supper, put on my gear, and we moved out into the bush, with Schwartz leading the way. We took it a little more carefully than usual that night, because we knew we weren't entering undefended territory. I was carrying the M-79 grenade launcher, and I had a buckshot round in it, and four extras on my belt.

For an hour or so nothing happened. Then, as Schwartz was moving quietly and carefully along a back trail, he stopped and held up his hand. He'd obviously heard something up ahead. He came back a few steps and motioned for me to join him. Then he put his finger to his lips. I heard them too—male voices. At this time of night they had to be Cong.

I signaled for the other three to move up, and as the five of us rounded the bend, we could see three huts barely visible in the thick darkness—a small village called Son Trang 4, one of the places where enemy activity was said to originate. Again we heard the men's voices, and we moved in closer. Suddenly there was silence.

Approaching the first hut I motioned Schwartz to step inside while the rest of us waited, weapons trained on the doorway. Schwartz came out hauling two women and two older boys. Then we went into the other two huts and brought out more women and children. Gathered in the darkness, they were no more than a black lump until the flashlight swept across their faces. Then we could see the widened eyes and grimly drawn mouths.

We stood them in the yard in front of the huts, ready to question them, while Schwartz checked back inside. The men were somewhere nearby, perhaps watching us from the jungle. We needed to move out quickly, and I went over to the door of the hut to get Schwartz out, wondering if he'd run into anybody inside.

Suddenly a bullet whizzed by my head, I saw a burst of fire, and heard a loud *thwack*, almost in the same instant. One woman reached under her pajamas while another made a sudden dash. There was another burst of fire.

"Shoot. Kill them all," I shouted, and fired the M-79, as the others blasted away. The grenade exploded in orange flame, and for the next ten seconds the night was lit with tracers. I could see flashes of fire behind the scattering Vietnamese as they stumbled and fell to the ground. Then, as quickly as it had begun, the firing was over, and silence surrounded us.

"Jesus!" I heard someone whisper out of the darkness.

"Let's get out of here!" I shouted.

We had to move out of the clearing as quickly as possible, because the enemy was somewhere in the jungle, peering in on us like someone looking into a lighted house from the darkness. So we ran back down the path, firing bursts into the darkness, wondering whether or not they were behind us. I held up my hand. We stopped, trying not to breathe while we listened. We heard them in the bush. They were coming.

"Move out!" I shouted, and we started running again, firing behind us as we ran. Then we stopped again, and we could still hear them behind us. So we left the trail and moved out into the bush, at least putting ourselves on an equal footing by using the jungle and the darkness as cover. Now no one was quite sure who was the cat and who was the mouse. For a couple of hours we played that game. I never knew how many were out there; but judging from the firepower I'd seen, we were outnumbered.

Finally, about an hour before dawn we made radio contact with the command post and Lieutenant Ambort ordered us in; so we slipped onto the trail and humped back into camp. Sergeant Meyer ran out to meet us.

"You guys all right? We heard the machine gun fire."

It was the first time I had known what kind of weapon had opened up on us. It's easy to tell the difference from a distance; but when they're right on you, sometimes it's impossible.

"We were ambushed," I said.

"Did you get any?" Meyer asked.

"We got some."

By then everyone on the team was worried about what had happened, though I didn't quite understand why, since we'd responded to an attack. As we walked into camp, Schwartz touched his neck with the tip of his fingers.

"Damn, that hurts."

I stopped and examined his neck. As soon as I saw it I knew what had happened.

"It's a bullet burn," I said. "That's the closest you'll ever come to being shot through the neck."

Then I looked him up and down. That's when I saw his rifle stock. It had been shattered —split in two by a bullet and rendered useless. So had he even fired his weapon? It's a question I still don't know the answer to, though I'd guess he hadn't.

He looked at it in bewilderment.

"I don't even remember that happening."

"It was when they first opened fire," I said, thinking he would remember, but he seemed puzzled.

"What are we going to say?" one of the others said.

"God! We killed a bunch of civilians. Women and children."

"We were fired on in the dark. Just tell the truth," I said. "Tell them you followed orders. I said 'fire' and you fired. Then they'll come to me. Don't worry. There's not going to be any trouble."

We called in artillery fire on the whole area, and soon we could hear the shells whistling in and exploding. The gun crews weren't firing at anyone in particular, just lobbing rounds into the sector in order to kill anything moving. That particular sector, known for Cong activity, had long ago been designated fair game, both for artillery fire and for bombing raids. By agreement with the government of South Vietnam, anyone killed in such raids was expendable.

Lieutenant Ambort came up and called me aside.

"What happened?" he asked. "Are you all right? Did you get any?"

I hesitated for a moment, knowing how eager he was to hear we'd paid them back for Sergeant Lyons.

"We were ambushed," I said. "We killed about five of them, I think."

It was a lie, or at best a half truth; and I would live to regret it. But at the moment I didn't have the heart to tell him we probably hadn't killed any Cong, though we might have blown away some women and children.

Later, after talking with one or two of the others, he must have found out the truth; because the next morning, when he reported the incident over the radio, he said we'd captured a rifle. He wanted to protect us, I guess, hoping the detail of the rifle would stave off an investigation. So he'd told a small lie, too—understandable, maybe, but in the long run one more mistake to contend with.

That morning, just after daylight, Lieutenant Lloyd Grant, an intelligence officer with just a few weeks in-country, took a team into the field to reconnoiter. He did not expect or intend to engage the enemy. He just wanted to scout the land and report back to battalion about the terrain and the difficulties we'd encountered over the past week. During the daytime the Vietcong were working in the fields or sacked out in their grass shacks and the women steered clear of all Americans, so he was a little surprised to see a young woman approaching, pointing behind her, and talking. One of the men with Lieutenant Grant translated her story into English.

They followed her to the village of Son Trang 4, where Lieutenant Grant had his first experience with the grimmer side of war. He saw dead bodies strewn all over the ground—bodies of women and children—and he was understandably shaken by the sight.

After talking to the Marines with him, he must have found out that our killer team had been in the area the night before and had reported an encounter with the enemy. He put two and two together and came to what he thought was four: We had simply mowed them down in revenge for the death of our own men.

At this point his horror turned to anger, and he returned to LZ Ross by helicopter, where he wrote a hot, strongly worded report, protesting the murder of innocent civilians and demanding that the incident be investigated. It is difficult to tell how important his letter was in determining what subsequently happened. But I'm inclined to think it made a big difference that he felt the way he did and expressed his feelings in such strong language.

Unaware that anything was going on, I was preparing to receive my Silver Star, with only the slightest twinge of conscience for not telling Lieutenant Ambort what had happened in more precise detail. But I was so certain that what we'd done was justified by the circumstances that I didn't even bother to get the team together and coordinate our stories. When you're in enemy territory at night and something moves, you fire instinctively, assuming that your life is in danger. Besides, we'd been shot at first. So I wasn't prepared for what followed.

The first thing I knew, Lieutenant Ambort came over and told me that the company had been called back from our command post, that there would be an investigation of what had happened at Son Trang 4. At that point I told him the whole truth, and he seemed to accept my explanation as perfectly in order.

When we landed back at LZ Ross, however, I began to realize that I might be in some trouble. We were met by a couple of Criminal Investigation Division officers and told that instead of going back to the huts, the five of us would be detained separately in five of the six guard towers that surrounded the base's high fence. These towers were no more than small lookout posts that commanded the countryside, one small jail where each of us could sweat it out.

After I'd settled in and was looking out across the clearing to the jungle, one of the CID officers, a captain, came up the steps, followed by a corporal with a notebook and a pencil. The captain came in with a sympathetic smile on his face, ready to do a job on me.

"Look, Corporal," he said, "we understand what you did. You gunned down those people because of what happened to your buddies. So just tell us that and we can close the book on this one. Nothing's going to happen to you. It won't

even go on your record. We just need to know
the truth so we can know what to tell the ARVNs
and the civilian authorities."

"Nice try, Captain," I told myself. "But I'm
not that big a fool."

So I carefully told him what had happened,
trying not to omit any of the details, since I
knew that if the others just stuck to the truth, all
the smaller pieces would fall into place. But the
captain wasn't buying my story.

"Come on, Marine! That's not what happened and you know it! You went in there,
rousted those people out, and then shot them
down. That's what the others are saying. All you
have to do is tell the truth. But if you don't, then
we'll throw the goddamned book at you. You understand!"

I assured him over and over again that we'd
been attacked, that the civilians had made the
moves, that we'd fired instinctively, just the way
we were trained.

He tried everything—threats, the buddy-
buddy approach, legal gobbledygook—but I
stuck to my story because I knew it would be
dangerous to make up some lie just to give him
what he wanted. After he'd left, however, I was
more than a little worried about what the others
might do. Not Green and probably not Schwartz
—I'd fought beside them and I knew what they
were made of. But I didn't know much about
either Boyd or Krichten. I just hoped they
weren't easily intimidated.

The investigation took a couple of days, and
other officers questioned me, trying to get me to
admit that the whole thing had been planned be-
forehand, that it was a particularly well-orches-

trated retaliation for the death of Lyons and the others. Again I stuck to the facts, but toward the end I began to believe them when they said the others were telling a different story.

Finally it was over. I was sleeping on the floor when I heard a helicopter crank up, then sweep off into the air. A CID officer came stumping up the steps to tell me the outcome of the investigation. He had an armed guard with him, so I guessed what was coming, though I wasn't really prepared for the nature of the charges.

"Corporal Herrod," he said, "we've finished our investigation, and we've concluded that you should be arrested and bound over for trial. The charges, in case you're interested, will be sixteen counts of premeditated murder."

He stepped forward and asked me to hold out my hands. When I did, he clapped handcuffs on my wrists. Then I walked down the wooden steps with the guard and CID officer following behind. What I saw next unnerved me even more. Twenty armed guards were waiting for me—ten to guard me on each side.

"This isn't happening," I told myself. "It can't be happening."

I was flown to Da Nang and taken to the brig, where I learned from somebody that four of us were being charged with murder and that Krichten had been given immunity to testify against us. I still didn't understand why they wanted to give us trouble and why the maximum charges.

What I didn't realize was the degree to which the top brass in the Marine Corps had been intimidated by the American press.

The My Lai cover-up had just come to light. The Army was catching hell for it. Lieutenant Calley was headline news. And now the Marines had an opportunity to wash their dirty linen in public, and in so doing, "one-up" the Army.

Later, during the course of my trial, my attorneys would obtain "stipulations" (summaries) of official communications ordering my conviction. But at the time none of it really made sense to me. I kept saying, "They can't do this to me."

DEEP LOCK

SCHWARTZ, BOYD, AND Green were already in the brig, having been taken out of LZ Ross just before I was; but I wasn't put in a proper cell immediately. Instead I was stashed in a cage at the receiving center. This cage was made out of chicken wire and two-by-fours. It was six feet by six feet, and when I lay down on the floor, I had to curl up. They kept me in there for three days without letting me out, except to go to the bathroom.

Then the desk sergeant, realizing how cramped I was, asked me if I'd like to work outside the confines of the chicken wire.

"I'll give you a choice," he said. "Stay in there and do nothing, or come out here and clean weapons."

"I'll clean anything just to stretch my legs," I said.

So I sat at a table, carefully cleaning shotguns, happy to be doing something that would take my mind off the ordeal I was facing.

Toward afternoon I was looking down a barrel to see if I'd missed any oil when a captain walked in, glanced at me, and then did a double take. He started dancing around, shouting at the sergeant.

"What in hell is this man doing outside that cage with a shotgun in his hand? Are you out of your mind? The son of a bitch is charged with killing 16 people! You want us to be 17th and 18th?"

I felt sorry for the sergeant, who knew perfectly well that I didn't pose any threat to him. The captain probably knew it too. But he had a point. I was politically hot, and somebody higher up might come in there and find me loose on the world.

I'm not sure why I ended up in solitary confinement. It wasn't my fault that I'd been found outside my cage, cradling a shotgun. Maybe with the sensitivity of the Son Trang 4 story it was smart to put me in the deepest dungeon they could find. One thing was certain—where I was, no reporter was likely to stumble on me by mistake. The My Lai massacre was the lead story on CBS News those days, and in retrospect I have to believe that the Marines wanted to keep control of my story, using it in just the right way to create the impression that they were honest and objective in dealing with war crimes.

When you live in a 7-foot-by-4-foot room for 22 days you face problems you've never encountered before. In the first place, the physical dimensions of the room severely limit your options for carrying out the basic functions of life. Food—the worst selection of C-rations possible—was brought in three times a day, a tray handed through the doorway. The guard did not speak, and I wasn't supposed to speak to him. When I finished my meal, I rapped on the door, and he picked up the tray—again in silence.

Of course these cramped quarters meant the worst possible bathroom arrangements—a "honey pot" that I could either put at the head of the pallet or at the foot. No choice, really; because even at the foot of my mattress the pot was 50 feet too close, and I had to live much of the time in the atmosphere of my own excrement.

When I entered the cell, they had already taken away my utility shirt and pants, my belt, and even the laces of my boots. There was one light in the middle of the ceiling, and it burned twenty-four hours a day. Since there was no window in the cell, I lived under perpetual artificial light, and only mealtimes enabled me to distinguish day from night.

I couldn't even unscrew the bulb when I was ready to go to sleep, because it was shielded by chicken wire that covered the entire ceiling. I suspect these precautions were not so much for the protection of guards as for the prevention of suicide by prisoners. Someone might well figure out a way to electrocute himself if he could unscrew the bulb and get his fingers into the socket.

I never considered killing myself, but I did think of everything else under the sun. First and foremost I thought about what I was facing—sixteen counts of premeditated murder. If I were convicted, I was reasonably certain I'd be sentenced to the maximum penalty, which was death. When I considered the fact that the charges had been preferred in the first place, I had to believe that the Marines would probably convict me, since they were already in possession of the essential facts, and were still going ahead with the trial.

I knew how the Uniform Code of Military Justice worked: you were guilty until proven innocent. The fact that I was in that cell, not much bigger than a casket, was a perfect illustration of the system in action. I was being held without charges, incommunicado, and I hadn't had the first glimpse of a lawyer. So I figured I was already on that old railroad, chugging down the track, with a firing squad waiting at the end of the line.

At least that's what my reason told me when I allowed myself to think about it. But my heart said something else. I had spent a year facing danger and death. Each new situation had seemed worse than the one before—boot camp, the DMZ, LZ Ross, and now this. In the past I'd adapted and survived. I had eaten that Last Supper of chicken and rice more times than I could count. And there I sat, still alive, probably finished with combat, with only one more big hurdle to jump. So somehow I believed I would get over this one too. When you're twenty years old, you don't believe anything can kill you, not even your own all-powerful government.

So I was optimistic as long as I didn't think about my case too long. In order to get my mind off the upcoming ordeal I thought about a variety of other things. I would try to remember incidents from high school. Then I'd think of my family and friends—my mother, my grandparents, girls I'd dated, even boot camp buddies, who learned at the same time I did the first and greatest lesson the Marine Corps teaches—how to kill.

In fact, the more I thought about my military training, the more absurd these charges became. What happened at that three-hut village, covered by darkness, was the culmination of everything I'd been trained to do. By the time I took that killer team out on that particular mission, I was almost the perfect Marine by boot-camp standards—conditioned in every way to respond to hostile actions in the field, an experienced technician in the craft of death. If you took the circumstances surrounding the incident at Son Trang 4 and presented them to trainees as a textbook problem in night fighting, the right answer to the problem would be to do what we'd done. I knew that in my bones as much as in my head, because I'd learned my lessons well at San Diego.

But I didn't let myself dwell on such thoughts for long; and after a while, when I couldn't stand remembering the past anymore, I did a variety of other things, some of them insane. For one thing, I became a cockroach watcher. For the first two or three days I simply killed the roaches and piled them in a neat little pyramid a few inches from my honey pot, thinking that maybe someday I would kill so many that they'd fill up the cell. Then I decided I'd study them, see if I could figure out what they did. I'd try to predict which way they'd turn, when they'd stop, and when they'd start again. Second-guess them when I could.

I counted the number of concrete blocks in the cell walls, and every single hole in the chicken wire—not once, but a number of times, until I got to the point where I always came up with the same number. Then it wasn't fun anymore.

Of course, I got mail from my grandparents and from Kay. But my mail was censored, both incoming and outgoing, so I'd receive letters with huge sections blacked out, probably because of references to the trial.

Once a week I was allowed to take a shower, which was my only time outside the cell. I'd be marched upstairs and outside to a wooden shower stall in the compound yard. There I'd be given soap, a washrag, and a towel (all paid for by deductions from my pay) and then I would be allowed to step into the shower for about a minute—just enough time to soap down and rinse off.

On the way back I'd be subjected to a "body cavity search" during which someone (maybe a doctor) would slip on a rubber glove, give me a rectal examination, and then peer down my throat with a flashlight. Then I would return to the cell, where I would begin to sweat again; and within an hour I would be just as gamy as I was before I took the shower. So it was hardly worth the trouble.

One day the door to my cell opened and I saw a hand holding something that looked like a hamburger. I couldn't believe it. A miracle. Then a grinning face peered around the edge of the door.

"Herrod, you should have stayed in Sydney instead of coming back to this man's Marine Corps."

It was Al Hafer from Myrtle Beach, South Carolina.

"Hafer," I said, "how did you get down in this hell hole?"

"I'm your new guard," he said. "And don't talk so loud. I'm not supposed to say a word to you because you're a dangerous killer."

We talked very quietly for the next few days, because officers would come by from time to time. I told him what had happened at Son Trang 4, and he told me what was happening with the others, that Krichten had made some sort of deal with the prosecution and would testify against the rest of us. I told him I didn't blame Krichten at this point, that he was smart to save his own ass.

We also reminisced about training days and about Sydney, so for a few days it wasn't so bad. Then one day an officer slipped up on us, chewed out Hafer, and the next day a guy I'd never seen before handed me a C-ration ham and eggs. The guy didn't say a word, and I didn't expect him to.

Finally it was over. The door opened, and a guard motioned me to follow him. No one explained to me that I was getting out of solitary confinement. They simply marched me back up to the receiving desk, where they gave me back my utilities, my belt, and my bootlaces and hustled me through the door—a guard in front of me, a guard behind.

It was when I moved outdoors that I began to realize I was finally out of solitary. By my own calculations—and I wasn't positive—I had been there one day over three weeks. Once again I had survived.

They marched me over to a detention barracks where ten or eleven other men were being held for trial. As I stepped through the door I looked around for Schwartz, Green, or any other familiar face—but no one I knew was there. Still, I figured it would be better than solitary. At least there would be other guys to talk to, and I could see several card games in progress, the participants sitting on footlockers or sprawled on the floor. No one was stretched out on a bunk, and I was immediately told that it was forbidden to lie down during the day.

Fortunately, I didn't spend much time in the detention barracks, though I was denied bail right from the beginning. So technically I was supposed to be handcuffed and chained whenever I left the barracks. Most of the other guys, whose cases were heard quickly, abided by the rules. But I was not brought to trial for six months, so I would have gone stir crazy if I'd had to stay in that small area for such a long period. And I had every reason to believe that's what I'd be doing— until the second day, when they told me I'd be seeing my military lawyer for the first time. I was handcuffed, a chain was put around my waist, and then I was driven by jeep to a building at the top of a steep hill—the Judge Advocate's Office. My "chaser" (guard) led me inside, where I saw a huge black man behind a desk. His name tag said "Sergeant Best," and I liked him from the moment I saw him.

As we entered the building he looked up at me, then at the chaser; and he pointed to a sign above the swinging doors that led into the lawyers' offices. The sign read: NO CHASERS BEYOND THIS POINT. So my chaser sat down, and

Sergeant Best motioned me to walk right on through the doors.

"First door on your left, Herrod," he said. "Captain's waiting for you."

I knocked, heard someone say "Come in," and stepped inside. Then I threw a salute.

The tall, thin black man laughed as he returned the salute.

"Boy, when you get into trouble you really do it, don't you?"

"Yes, sir," I said with a grin. "I really do."

It was Captain Williams, and already I felt better.

"Sit down," he said. "Light up if you want to. Tell me what the hell happened this time."

So I told him the story while he took notes on a yellow legal pad. I told him everything I remembered. I didn't leave out things that put me in a bad light, and I didn't add anything to the account. Every so often he would stop me to ask a question, then, after jotting down my answer, tell me to continue.

When I finished, he read over his notes, then put them aside and stared at me for a moment.

"Do we have a chance, sir?" I asked.

"What do you mean?" he said, wide-eyed. "You've got me on your side, don't you? Of course we have a chance! We're going to win this case!"

I might say here that Captain Williams was the only person involved in the case who thought I would be acquitted. Everyone else was convinced from the beginning that in order to get an acquittal we would have to get a change of venue or else win on appeal. But Williams—who had the best win record of any military de-

fense lawyer in the Judge Advocate's Office—
never thought he was going to lose the case. He
had faith in the system; but more than that, he
had faith in his own ability to out-think and out-
talk the opposition. So by the time he finished
outlining the information he would need in order to prepare for the trial, I was beginning to
share his confidence.

"How is life in the detention barracks?" he
asked.

"It beats the Deep Lock," I said.

"We'll try to get you out on bail," he said. "In
the meantime, I'm going to be needing you every
day. Or that's what we're going to say. You can
hang around here, write letters, listen to the radio, sleep—whatever you want to do. It'll be better than lying around on the floor all day, losing
your money to card sharps. And you can eat PX
chow instead of C-rations."

I couldn't believe my good luck; and for the
first time since I came down from the tower
back at LZ Ross, I felt like a member of the human race. At least I would be half free, even if I
couldn't leave Captain Williams's office.

But that wasn't the end of my good luck.
About a week later, when I showed up, I found
Lieutenant Ambort waiting for me. After we had
shaken hands, he told me why he was there.

"They're short of guards at the detention
barracks, and you're taking up a lot of their
time. I've fixed it so the members of your platoon will be guarding you."

"What will that mean?" I asked.

"At the very least it means you can relax a
little. Our guys are all on your side, so they won't
ride you."

That was an understatement. From that day forward I was free to move around the base, with the only stipulation that I have one of my own platoon members ride with me at all times. Each morning my chaser would arrive and sign me out to Captain Williams's office. Usually we would go there first and see if he needed me for anything or if he'd heard anything new. Then we would either hang around there or else move on to some recreational spot on the base. Sometimes we would go for a beer. And we rarely missed a new movie. I began to feel sorry for the poor guys back in detention barracks, but I kept my mouth shut because I figured if somebody upstairs found out, I might end up in the Deep Lock.

One day we almost blew the entire sweet setup. I had just been picked up by Rodrigucz, one of the guys in my platoon; and as he walked out to the jeep, he turned to me and asked if I wanted a Coke. I told him I did, fished some coins out of my pocket, and gave him change. Then I climbed into the jeep to wait for him.

The staff sergeant in the detention center happened to look out the window at just that moment and saw me sitting there, a satisfied grin on my face, with no one within 30 feet of me. As a matter of fact, from where he was standing, he couldn't see Rodriguez at all.

He came roaring out the door like a wounded bull, waving his pistol and shouting. About that time Rodriguez strolled back to the jeep, holding a Coke in each hand, a .45 in his holster. The sergeant started screaming at him. Then he ordered me out of the jeep, hauled me inside, slapped a pair of handcuffs on my wrists, and looped a chain around my neck.

"You get on back to your company," he snarled to Rodriguez. "I'll take charge of this prisoner."

He led me out to the jeep, and then climbed in and cranked it up. We rode in silence to the Judge Advocate's Office, stopped, and he turned to me.

"Get out and walk in front of me. And don't you make a move, you hear?"

I nodded and went silently, because I knew he could make life rough for me, but I was seething with anger. When we walked through the door, Sergeant Best looked up, and his eyes narrowed.

"Unlock him and then you sit down right there," he said, pointing to a chair near the NO CHASERS sign.

"The hell you say," the staff sergeant barked. "Regulations say that I go where he goes. And that's what I intend to do."

Best smiled and shrugged his shoulders.

"Suit yourself," he said. "But if you step through that swinging door, you'll wake up in front of this hooch and wonder how the hell you got there."

As he delivered this speech, Best rose like a mountain from behind the desk. I don't know whether or not the staff sergeant knew that Best was a fourth-degree black belt, but he obviously figured he couldn't cope with this quiet-spoken giant, so he slid into a chair and said nothing more.

In order to rub it in, I walked over and sat

behind one of the typewriters like I owned the place.

"I'm going to write a letter," I announced to Best, who nodded.

The staff sergeant knew the full ramifications of what I was doing. Letters by prisoners were censored; but if you wrote and mailed them outside of the detention center, no one could restrict what you said. It was a smart-ass gesture on my part, but I couldn't pass up the opportunity.

When Captain Williams came in, he sized up the situation immediately.

"Herrod," he said, "you and Best come with me to the back."

We followed him into the office and he asked me what was going on. After I told him, he shook his head; but he was smiling.

"You want that sergeant to climb on your back so Best here will flatten him, don't you?"

I grinned and nodded.

"Well, we can't have that."

He went out and ordered the staff sergeant back to the detention center. Then he made another call, and in a few minutes Rodriguez was back at the Judge Advocate's Office. That afternoon we stopped by the NCO club and drank a couple of beers, then caught a movie.

A few days later, on a weekend, the same staff sergeant came into the detention barracks, looked around, saw me, and motioned me to the door. This was not a work day and I wouldn't be seeing Captain Williams till Monday, so I figured I'd had it. I went over to him quietly.

"Herrod," he said between clenched teeth, "your grandfather's here to see you."

I shook my head.

"A funny joke, Sergeant."

"It's no joke," the sergeant said. "He's right upstairs waiting for you. I got orders to take you up."

I was immediately suspicious. I figured he was going to take me somewhere and work me over.

"What does my grandfather look like?" I asked.

"Uh, short, heavy-set, white hair cut short. Has glasses."

It sounded right, but that was a description of anybody's grandfather, so I was still uncertain.

"What is he wearing?"

"Gray suit."

"Is he wearing anything else?"

"No. Except he's got a hat on."

I couldn't believe it! But as soon as he said "hat," I knew it had to be true. My grandfather was old-fashioned and would never be seen out of the house without his hat. It wasn't a matter of keeping his head warm. It was a matter of being completely dressed.

When I entered the room and saw him, his face a little older than I had remembered it, I almost broke down. It had been a long time since I'd seen a close friend, much less someone from my family. I threw my arms around him and probably cracked a few of his ribs.

Then I was aware that a man was standing next to him, and my grandfather introduced us.

"Randy, this is Senator Gene Stipe from Oklahoma. He's come all the way over here to help defend you."

I shook hands with Gene Stipe.

"And that's not all," my grandfather said. "Senator Denzil Garrison is coming too. He's the minority leader of the State Senate. They're both going to help you."

Stipe was a tall, stocky man with brown hair and a widow's peak. He had a good smile and a strong grip, and I liked him from the start. In his mid-forties, he was already a well-known trial lawyer in Oklahoma and a rising star in Democratic politics.

During the many hours we were to spend together, I learned that he was both a brilliant legal tactician and a tireless worker. One year, when he was a young man, he had worked as a fireman to put himself through law school and was running for the state legislature at the same time. At the end of the year, he'd passed the bar, been elected to the Oklahoma House, and had helped put out a lot of fires.

I was grateful to have him on my side. He was there as a volunteer, paying his own way to Vietnam—no small expense. In fact, before the trial had ended, he would make the trip overseas twice more, and his total out-of-pocket expenses would total over $25,000. He came, he said, because he believed in his responsibility to serve the people of his senatorial district—and I was one of those people. (When I came back to Oklahoma and had the opportunity to vote in my first election, I didn't spend too much time thinking about a choice for state senator.)

Gene and my grandfather told me that I had all sorts of support back in my home state, that everybody was pulling for me. The city of Calvin had even raised the money for my grandfather

to come over and see me; and the two senators—
one a Democrat, the other a Republican—were
volunteering their services. So Captain Williams
would have two more lawyers to help him
gather and present evidence.

Again I told my story—this time to Gene
and my grandfather. Again the lawyer interrupted my narrative to ask me questions. But
unlike Captain Williams, he didn't take notes.
Yet when he went back over the testimony, he
remembered every detail of what I'd told him.

"You say you won the Silver Star?"

He turned to my grandfather.

"I haven't seen anything about that in the
newspapers."

"I was going to be presented with a medal
the day after I came back from Son Trang 4."

"What about witnesses?"

I named the others.

"I told them to tell the truth," I said. "They
probably told the investigators that I ordered
them to fire."

"Did you?" Gene asked.

"Yes, sir. I did."

"Anybody else around? Any of the Vietnamese?"

"I don't know," I said. "I don't think anyone
knows."

After we'd talked a little longer, we went
over to Captain Williams's office, where Gene
and my grandfather met him. They all got along
well. When Gene said he'd come to help out, the
captain seemed pleased. They compared notes
for a while, and Captain Williams was obviously
impressed with Gene's experience and grasp of
legal technicalities. Gene, after all, was already a

famous trial lawyer in the Southwest, with a number of successful murder trials under his belt, while Williams, a brilliant man, was just a couple of years out of law school and hadn't dealt with a case this big.

"Let's do it this way," Captain Williams finally said. "You head the defense and conduct the trial. I'll take over when there's anything of a military nature involved."

"Fair enough," said Gene, and they shook on it.

"I'll also try to pull a few strings in Washington," Gene said. "Maybe we can get these charges reduced or a change of venue."

Gene stayed around for a couple of days, trying to get answers to crucial questions; but the military authorities were resisting every step of the way. Gene was particularly anxious to make an on-site inspection of Son Trang 4, but the Marines refused to give him authorization, saying it was a combat zone and that civilians weren't allowed in, even under extraordinary circumstances.

However, when they denied him permission, he wasn't necessarily unhappy.

"They seem determined to convict," he said, as we were sitting in Captain Williams's office. "But if we don't whip them here, we can always do it in higher court. Forbidding us to investigate the site of the alleged crime would be excellent grounds for overturning a conviction."

Because he was getting nowhere, and because he had responsibilities back home, he gave up for the time being. He and my grandfather caught the plane back to the United States.

But not before Gene had promised to come back again as soon as he had the opportunity.

I said goodbye to my grandfather, wishing I'd taken his advice and gone on to college, instead of being so bull-headed and joining the Marines. I could see in his eyes how much pain this was causing him, and I felt worse about that than about my own situation.

When Gene got back to Oklahoma, he called a press conference to report on his trip; and the story made the national wires. People were following it along with the My Lai investigation, because both stories had become a part of the continuing debate over Vietnam—the wisdom of our being there, the reasons why we weren't winning.

During this press conference Gene mentioned the fact that I had been scheduled to receive the Silver Star for valor, and the next day the Pentagon issued a formal denial, saying that no such award had been approved, that their records showed no evidence of a recommendation. So the story made me look like a liar and Gene like a fool. When he tried to investigate further, the muckety-mucks in the Pentagon stuck by their denial.

However, the coverage, carried in newspapers across the country, accomplished something else that was extremely important: Lieutenant Oliver North learned that halfway around the world I was in trouble.

North, who was now a training officer at Quantico, immediately went to his commanding officer and said he had information pertinent to the trial. His C.O. listened to his story, then suggested that he get in touch with Captain Wil-

liams in Vietnam and Gene Stipe in Oklahoma.
So North wrote a letter to both men; and subsequently, Gene called North and talked to him at
great length.

Later Gene would say of his conversation
with Lieutenant North: "He said he would pay
his own way to the West Coast, then take a military hop to Vietnam. He'll appear as a character
witness and also back up your story about the
Silver Star. He's going to take leave time to do
this. You can't ask for more."

At the time I doubt either Gene or I fully
understood the degree to which North would influence the trial, not only on the witness stand in
my behalf, but also as an investigator. He more
than anyone else was able to cut through the red
tape and get answers to questions. It's not too
much to say that he risked his life for me as well
as his career, and in the end I would owe him
more than he ever owed me for those few seconds up on the top of Mutter's Ridge.

While I was waiting for my own case to be investigated, Schwartz, with only a military lawyer to
defend him, came to trial. Needless to say, I was
interested in the outcome because whatever evidence the prosecution presented against him
would undoubtedly reappear when my case was
heard. I figured the prosecution would be based
on what the five of us had said, and I fully expected to be called as a witness in defense of
Schwartz. As a matter of fact, I had even offered
to testify in his behalf, corroborating his story
and providing eye-witness testimony that he had
been grazed by a bullet and had his rifle butt
shattered.

As it turned out, Schwartz's defense had been based solely on the fact that I had given the order to fire—an accurate account of what had happened, though an incomplete one. What I didn't realize at the time was the degree to which all of the others—Schwartz, Green, Boyd, and Krichten—were still ignorant of the true sequence of events. Since their lawyers had not even questioned me, but had proceeded to build their own defenses without hearing the full story, no one really had enough information to put together a legitimate defense based on the fact that we had been fired on and were protecting our lives.

Instead, all the Marine lawyers—noncombatants themselves—had concluded precisely what Lieutenant Grant had concluded: that we had deliberately murdered innocent peasants, just as Lieutenant Calley had apparently done. The one case was influencing the other, and everyone was conditioned by what he'd read in the newspapers. So I should have anticipated the results of Schwartz's trial, but I didn't.

It took place in the same building where Lieutenant Williams's office was located; and day after day I saw the judge advocate, the seven-man jury panel, the prosecutor, Schwartz, and his lawyer all troop into the tiny courtroom and shut the door behind them. But I wasn't allowed in myself.

However, I did have representation at the trial. As he had promised, Gene Stipe returned with Denny Garrison, who was Republican leader of the Oklahoma Senate. Though Gene and Denny were on opposite sides of the political fence, they were good buddies and enjoyed kidding one another. While Gene was known as a great courtroom performer, Denny—stocky and slightly shorter, with graying temples—had a sharp investigative mind, and he had come to pore over the evidence and see what he could make of it. I was grateful for his presence, and over the next months he dug out many of the facts that Gene used in the courtroom, facts that Schwartz's lawyers failed to uncover, or even to look for.

Day after day Gene and Denny would come into Captain Williams's office, shaking their heads.

"I can't believe the defense," Denny said one day. "Today two Vietnamese women took the stand. They testified that they'd seen five Marines enter their village at night and that later they'd heard shots. That was all!"

"And Schwartz's attorney didn't even cross-examine them," Gene added incredulously.

Another day they reported on Krichten's testimony.

"He said Schwartz and Randy had fired by themselves, killing all sixteen of the people. Randy with one shot from his M-79 grenade launcher, Schwartz with his busted M-16 rifle. And that's their case!"

When Schwartz took the stand in his own behalf, he told about hearing me shout an order to fire, saying "Kill them all!" He claimed he obeyed the order instinctively, then realized that he was blasting away at civilians. So I was to blame, since he only obeyed orders without thinking, the way a good Marine is supposed to react.

"Are they going to convict him?" I asked

Gene and Denny. Suddenly I was beginning to feel knots in my stomach every time I thought about Schwartz's trial.

Denny shrugged his shoulders.

"The evidence is circumstantial, but, gee, his attorney has done a bad job. He hasn't really brought out the contradictions and ambiguities in the case. I really wouldn't care to call it now."

"Neither would I," said Gene.

Then one day it was over, and Gene and Denny came in, grim and tight-lipped, to tell me the verdict.

"Guilty. Twelve counts of premeditated murder. Unbelievable."

Later that day, the judge advocate sentenced Schwartz to 12 consecutive life terms, one for each of the civilians they arbitrarily said he murdered. So if they sentenced him to life for obeying my orders, then what would my sentence be for setting everything in motion? We all knew the answer to that question, though nobody came right out and said it.

Garrison had been spending most of his time scratching around, trying to interview everyone who had been either at Son Trang 4 or at the company command post. But it wasn't always easy to track guys down. Some had been rotated back to the States. Others had been transferred to other units. Still others were perpetually out in the field where Denny couldn't reach them. He began to suspect that someone was making his task deliberately difficult.

"There are plenty of unanswered questions," he said. "But maybe we'll do a little better when we come back for the trial. We'll try to get here a

few days early, but it's difficult to deal with the
military when you're on the outside looking in."

We said goodbye, and I went back to my
daily routine of hanging around the captain's office, drinking a few beers, or watching the latest
movie. It wasn't a bad life, but I was beginning
to feel that time was running out, that maybe
this would be the bullet I couldn't dodge.

Next Boyd was tried, and his attorney wouldn't
talk to me either, much less put me on the stand.
I'll say this: the defense they came up with was
imaginative. Boyd got on the stand and testified
that he'd been a conscientious objector, that during his entire tour of duty he had never attempted to kill a Vietnamese.

What had he done that night?

"I deliberately fired over their heads," he
said.

I heard all of this secondhand, and I had
known him just long enough to be reasonably
certain he was lying. But I didn't blame him for
trying anyway, particularly after Schwartz's
conviction. I must admit I was bowled over by
the verdict: "Not guilty!"

Why, after all, would a conscientious objector spend his entire tour of duty being shot at by
Vietcong when he could have announced his res-
ervations and been reassigned? The prosecutor
should have been able to rip him to shreds.
Later, however, when he showed up as a prosecution witness at my trial, I understood why
they probably went light on him in cross-examination.

* * *

Then came Green, who stuck to the truth, despite what had happened to Schwartz. While I didn't blame the others for trying any trick to beat the rap, I felt particularly bad about Green, who had always fought well and who was doggedly doing what he thought was right, even though he knew it wouldn't work. Because the Marines had already concluded that Schwartz and I had killed all sixteen of the dead, they charged Green with unpremeditated murder, arguing that he was an accessory; and they prosecuted the case with the same ruthless intensity they'd shown in the Schwartz trial. So Green was convicted and sentenced to five years and a dishonorable discharge.

Meanwhile, my case was moving toward a trial date; and Gene and Denny, who were beginning to believe I was being railroaded, were frantically pulling strings to get a change of venue. Gene went to Washington and talked to Carl Albert, then Speaker of the House, and Albert put him in touch with Mendel Rivers, Chairman of the Armed Services Committee, and the most powerful man in the country where military affairs were concerned.

Rivers was the man who decided which branch of the service got what appropriations; so when he wanted a favor, the military was usually happy to oblige him. In this case, however, nothing was done, either because Rivers didn't push it or because the Marines dug in their heels and refused to give ground.

When Gene and Denny arrived back in Vietnam for the trial, they brought an invasion force of their own. They had already decided that in view of Schwartz's conviction and their failure to get a change of venue, they were going to have a tough time winning on the Marines' home field. So they were preparing to file an appeal if we lost. Consequently, they brought the best appeals lawyer in the state of Oklahoma, Harry Palmer. He was as tall as Gene, but slimmer and more angular. A corporate lawyer in Oklahoma City, he spoke softly and logically at all times. Gene and Denny told me that Harry would be taking notes during the trial and advising Gene on strategies that might later result in a reversal.

The second BNG was Dick Miller, who was there to search the law books for whatever rulings and precedents Gene and Denny needed. A quiet man, he wore glasses and had light hair cut in a flat-top. He had been a victim of polio, and in addition to the braces on his legs, he also used two aluminum crutches that were attached to his arms. On level ground he moved around quite well, but he obviously had great difficulty on an incline, and I wondered how he would be able to climb up and down the steep hill to court every day.

Dick was the best legal researcher in the business; and like Gene, Denny, and Harry, he had volunteered for this tour and had paid his own expenses.

After I had met everyone, I began to feel more confident about my chances. Schwartz and Green clearly hadn't been so lucky; and if I had harbored any resentment against the system for what had happened to me, it was lost in the gratitude I felt toward these men, who had come thousands of miles to help a perfect stranger.

At this point I had the best possible defense team, and I was ready to stand trial.

THE RETURN OF NORTH

FOR MONTHS I'D been straining to get into court so I could set the record straight. First I'd volunteered to be a witness in the trials of Schwartz, Boyd, and Green—the men who had been with me on the patrol. Then I'd prayed for my own trial to begin. But as soon as I walked through the door and saw the size of the courtroom I knew I was going to be sorry.

In the first place, the whole building—a Quonset hut with a cement floor—was no more than 24 feet long and 16 feet wide, the dimensions of a fair-sized bedroom. Under ordinary circumstances the space would have been overcrowded with the judge advocate, a bailiff, a court stenographer, seven jurors, the prosecutor, the defense lawyer, and the defendant. But in addition to this minimal number, my team of volunteer attorneys from Oklahoma numbered four; and just so he wouldn't be outgunned, the prosecutor brought in three extra assistants. Also, eight members of the press were jammed together on the two back benches. So counting everybody, there were 28 of us in the room when the trial was in full swing, all of us inhal-

ing the same meager supply of oxygen and ex-
haling clouds of carbon dioxide. There were no
windows. It was August. The temperature was
easily 110 degrees. And the only thing we had to
cut the heat was a single ceiling fan that churned
the air just enough to keep a swarm of flies from
settling.

Each morning as we entered at the rear we
found ourselves in an aisle that bisected the
room. At the back we saw two rows of hard-
wood benches on either side of the aisle, like
pews in a country Baptist church. Ordinarily
both rows were reserved for spectators, but the
press could use only the rear benches because
my four civilian lawyers filled up the second
row on the left and the three extra prosecutors
filled up all but one seat on the right. In front of
the benches on the left stood two oak tables for
the defendant and on the right the same number
for the prosecution. The judge advocate presided
over the trial from a desk perched on a raised
platform, and in front of him were two chairs
where the bailiff and stenographer sat. The witness stand was no more than a low platform in
front of the defendant with a chair on it, and the
seven jurymen lined up across the back wall facing the prosecution and defense, separated by a
wooden fence.

At some point during the trial it occurred to
me that the judge advocate was located on the
prosecutor's side of the aisle rather than in the
middle—a fact I thought was significant. With
that arrangement, the judge and prosecutors
formed a small, intimate group in a separate sector of the room, as if among the five of them

they would ultimately decide what was to be done with me. I asked Gene and Denny if they'd noticed the same thing, and they smiled grimly and nodded their heads.

The judge advocate was a Navy commander, a man in his middle forties with short brown hair. I guessed he'd been an athlete when he was younger, because of the way he moved and carried himself; but his body had thickened in middle age, and in a few years he would be fat. Throughout the trial his green Navy utilities were dark with sweat.

The head of the jury was an older man with cropped hair and graying temples, a bird colonel in the Marines. His name was Millard Blue, and he was a legitimate combat hero, having been decorated in both World War II and in Korea. He and the other six jurors sat throughout the trial with implacable faces, as if they were concentrating on a tactical problem rather than deciding the fate of a fellow human being. For the first few days I kept looking up at them to see how they were reacting to testimony, but after a while I gave up. They never broke to smile or even to yawn near the end of the day. I particularly watched one balding lieutenant colonel who had a steel plate in the back of his head—a result of a round he'd caught at Cho Sen Reservoir in Korea. I was counting on him to see things my way, and I thought at one crucial point in Lieutenant North's testimony he might have nodded his head just once, but I couldn't be absolutely positive, and he certainly didn't do it again. At the end of the trial, when they retired to deliberate, I had absolutely no idea of what was going on in their heads.

Eleven days of intensive cross-examination and verbal exhange took their toll on all of us, and there were moments in that infernal heat, sweat dripping off the end of my nose, when I was ready to stand up and admit I was guilty, just to feel a real breeze and get away from the press of other people. But those moods came rarely and didn't last long. It's amazing how much physical discomfort you can forget when you are standing trial for your life and your fate hangs on every word a witness is speaking. So for that reason I probably had an easier time than the others, all of whom suffered equally in the intense heat, where the fan did nothing more than distribute the hot air evenly around the room. (Years later, when my wife explained to me what a convection oven was, I told her I'd spent 11 days in one.)

The members of the press were luckier. There must have been 50 of them there to cover what turned out to be one of the ten top news stories of the year. But there were only eight seats in those two benches that formed the back row, so most of them had to remain outside— the fortunate ones. They devised a rotation system that seemed to work quite well. Eight would start out in the seats at the beginning of the day. These would stay for a while and then surrender their positions to eight more from the huge pool waiting outside. The AP, UPI, the three networks, and the major newspapers were represented; as well as several Oklahoma papers and television stations.

Every morning when I walked into the Quonset hut they would be there, cameras grinding, microphones jabbing, questions flying, strobe lights adding their heat to the already overpowering heat of the day. And when I walked out at lunchtime and at 5 P.M., they would be there waiting with the same questions and the same electronic gadgets. My lawyers told me to smile at the cameras and ignore the questions, so I did.

And that's how things generally went for the 11 days of the trial; but of course each day was different, with its own set of problems and surprises. It never occurred to me that so much new evidence would be uncovered while the trial was going on, or that things would turn out the way they did.

The first day I met with my five attorneys in Captain Williams's office, and together we walked across the black-topped road to the courtroom. Ten or twelve reporters were already hanging around the front door, dressed in short-sleeved Hawaiian shirts, holding notebooks or cradling hand-cameras. I was trying to remain cool and to laugh at the jokes Gene and Denny were cracking, but approaching the courtroom for the first time was probably the toughest moment I experienced until Colonel Millard Blue stood up in the courtroom to announce the jury's verdict. As I looked at the tiny Quonset hut just before I entered, it occurred to me that one day soon I might be led out that very same door in handcuffs, on my way to the brig and then, a little later, to a firing squad, which was the way they executed American servicemen sentenced to death in Vietnam.

The reporters stood back and I entered first, followed by Dick on his crutches, then Captain

Williams and Harry and Dennis and Gene. I was
surprised to see the room empty. I glanced at my
watch. It was a few minutes before 9 A.M., and
no one else was in sight. Five minutes later the
bailiff, the stenographer, and the prosecutor had
arrived. Then the other prosecutors. Finally,
from the back of the room a voice barked out:
"Ten-shun," and the judge advocate entered and
marched down the aisle. I checked my watch
again. It was 9:00 on the dot.

The voice at the back of the room belonged
to the sergeant-at-arms, whose job it was to control traffic in and out of the building. It was he
who brought prospective jurors into the courtroom, where they would sit in the witness chair,
sweat, answer questions posed by several prosecutors and defense lawyers, then either be accepted or rejected.

I watched carefully, trying to determine precisely what criteria Denny and Gene were using
to pick these men, most of whom seemed grim-
lipped and cold-blooded. I wondered if they
were making any mistakes, but I kept my mouth
shut, figuring they knew what they were doing,
even if I didn't. This procedure lasted for one
full day and half of a second, and we rejected
several prospects that seemed good bets to me. I
thought they appeared to be a little more hu-
mane.

Finally, at the end of the second morning—
after all seven had been picked and Gene,
Denny, Captain Williams, and I were lounging
around in the captain's cubicle—I asked them
how they thought we had done.

They were pleased.

"We've got seven combat officers on the

jury," Gene told me. "That means every one of them will know what it's like to be in the field under tremendous stress. I'd say we accomplished quite a bit."

"Is that what you were looking for?" I asked.

"That and some indication of fairness, a willingness to weigh both sides of a question," said Captain Williams. "I think we got seven first-rate men. The better men they are, the more likely they'll be willing to weigh their own experience in deciding if what you did was justified."

"What about picking a couple of guys with a little more heart?" I asked.

"Emotions are unpredictable," said Denny. "A bleeding heart might feel sorry for you. Then again, he might feel even sorrier for those 16 women and children you guys allegedly murdered."

"You got a point," I said.

The more I thought about it the more it made sense, but it meant I had to live with those stoney faces for the next nine days, and I felt an additional chill in my marrow. Suddenly all of this was getting scary again.

Gene, Denny, and Captain Williams began reviewing their notes on the jurors, and I sat there, half-listening, wondering for the thousandth time how it would all turn out. Just when I was beginning to feel sorry for myself, a head popped around the partition of the cubicle.

"How are things going?"

It was Lieutenant Ambort, and he was in a decidedly upbeat mood. Then he looked at me.

"Why are you so down in the mouth?" he said, and whacked me on the shoulder. I jumped up, grabbed him, and we wrestled around the

room, laughing and gasping while the three lawyers enjoyed the sport. We knocked a couple of
chairs down, and finally ended up on the floor,
with me on top of Lieutenant Ambort, hands on
his throat.

Suddenly a shadow fell across the gray concrete, and we both froze and looked up at the
same instant. A figure filled the entrance of the
cubicle, and somone stared down at us with cold
blue eyes.

It was Lieutenant Oliver North.

We both scrambled to our feet and stood
there sheepishly, like a couple of kids. For some
reason I can't explain, you just didn't do things
like that around him. It was a "presence" you
felt—and not only after you'd served under him.
Lieutenant Ambort felt it as well.

Lieutenant North smiled, offered his hand,
and I shook it, remembering the surprising
strength of his grip.

"Thanks for coming," I said.

"I wouldn't have missed it," he said.

Then I introduced him to Lieutenant
Ambort, Gene, Denny, and Captain Williams;
and Lieutenant Ambort dragged in another
chair from the next cubicle.

"Any of the guys from the old platoon still
around?" Lieutenant North asked me as he sat
down in a wooden folding chair.

I told him I hadn't seen any of them in
about six months, because I'd been in the brig.

"Well, I'm glad you didn't run into any of
them there," he said with a grin.

Gene glanced at his watch.

"Lieutenant," he said, "it's almost one

o'clock. Would you like to get something to eat first, or are you ready to get to work?"

"Let's get on it," Lieutenant North said, and suddenly I realized that my mood had changed. The creeping despair of the last two days had disappeared. I knew then that I had a chance, perhaps even a good chance, though I didn't really know what difference North might make.

"These are our main problems," Gene said. "First, we don't know anything about the scene where this incident took place, except what Randy can remember—and he was only there for a few minutes in the dark of night. We've asked for permission to visit the site, and we've been turned down. Not once, but three times. On the other hand, the prosecution has access, and they have a witness: Lieutenant Grant, who led a reconnaissance patrol into the village a day after the incident and made fairly extensive notes on what he saw. We need our own eyewitness and the answers to some crucial questions."

North nodded, but I wasn't sure whether he was just signaling that he understood or whether he was suggesting he could pull some strings and get us into Son Trang 4.

"Second," said Gene, "Randy's certain that one of the guys on that patrol was grazed by enemy fire and that the stock of his rifle was shattered by an enemy bullet. If we could prove it, I think we could turn the whole case around. But we need the weapon."

North looked puzzled.

"I don't understand," he said. "That should all be a matter of ordnance records. Simplest thing in the world to check and see if the stock was replaced."

"There's just one problem," Denny said. "Both the rifle and the records have disappeared. It seems nobody can locate them."

North raised his eyebrows and looked over at Captain Williams.

"The Marines have misplaced a rifle?"

Captain Williams shrugged his shoulders.

"That's what they claim," he said.

I could tell Lieutenant North knew something was rotten, but he wasn't making any accusations—not yet.

"Third," Gene continued, "we'll need some help in locating witnesses. Some of the guys who know what happened that night have already been shipped back to the States, but most are still stashed somewhere. The Marines haven't exactly broken their necks to help us round up our witnesses. You might be able to help with that too."

"How much time do we have?" North asked.

"We picked the last juryman this morning," Denny said. "Trial resumes tomorrow morning. We've got maybe four or five days before we have to put our own witnesses on the stand. But some of this information would be useful in cross-examining the prosecution's witnesses."

There was a moment of silence as we all looked at one another.

"The bastards haven't given us enough information to prepare this case," said Denny with sudden anger. "We'll eat them alive on appeal, but right now we're in need of help."

I watched Gene and Denny as they stared at North, trying to communicate something without words. I wasn't sure what it was, but later that afternoon I found out. North looked from one to the other, then held his palms up in a questioning gesture.

"Okay," he said. "What do you need first?"

"Well, "said Gene, "how about your trying to persuade some old buddy to get us back into Son Trang 4."

"That shouldn't be too hard," said North, checking his watch. "How far is it from here?"

Everyone looked at me.

"About fifty kilometers," I said. "An hour's drive in a jeep."

North turned to Captain Williams.

"Do you suppose you could get me wheels for a day or two?"

"No problem," said Captain Williams. "When do you want them?"

"Right now," said North.

In less than an hour he was on his way; but before he left he and the lawyers had taken out pencil and paper to map strategy, as if they were preparing for a major military offensive. Lieutenant North and Denny Garrison would investigate all leads and try to answer tough questions, like what happened to Schwartz's gun, what kind of people lived in Son Trang 4, how many other guys heard the machine gun fire that Sergeant Meyer heard, and what bullets were actually found in the bodies of the victims.

Dick would be looking for military cases (if any) where armed forces personnel had been tried on similar charges and acquitted. Harry Palmer would draw up a list of grounds for appeal and make certain the investigation would center on those points. And Gene and Captain Williams would be taking all this information, digesting it, and building a case to present in the courtroom. As for me, when I wasn't in the courtroom I was to "stay put" in the office so I would be available to answer any questions.

As soon as North had left for the motor pool, with Lieutenant Ambort as his guide, Gene turned to Captain Williams.

"Do you think he's for real?"

"I think he's for real," Williams said. "I think we're home free now, so I'm going over to the Officers's Club and hoist a few. Either of you non-enlisted men care to join me?"

Gene and Denny shook their heads and watched quietly as he left. They had that look again, the one I noticed on their faces when they were talking to North, and I didn't like it.

"Okay," I said. "What's up? Obviously you know something I don't know. So what is it?"

They exchanged glances. Then they sighed and told me the facts of life.

"It's going to be hard for you to understand this, Randy," said Denny, "but some cases are meant to be won at trial and some on appeal. This case is going to be won on appeal. We haven't had a chance to examine the site of the action. We haven't had a chance to interview key witnesses. Evidence has disappeared. Deals have obviously been made. We haven't even been given a ballistics report on the victims, since no one bothered to have the bodies examined. We've been denied our request to exhume the bodies. In addition, you were held incommunicado for 22 days during a period when much of this evidence should have been gathered."

"Any one of these things might result in an overturned verdict," Gene explained, "but all to-

gether they make a reversal a certainty. So don't
you worry."

I thought about that a moment, trying to
make sure I had it right.

"In other words, you're telling me we're going to lose this trial," I said.

They paused, looked at each other, then
nodded at me.

"That's about it," said Gene.

"No chance in the world?"

"None. But the odds are heavy we'll win on
appeal. You just need to prepare for the inevitable. You've got to accept the idea that you're going to hear yourself pronounced guilty and
sentenced to death."

When I heard him say this, my gut
wrenched and I felt a little queasy.

"And you're telling me not to worry?"

"That's right," said Denny. "In the long run
we can't lose."

I thought about what he was saying, and it
seemed logical enough; but it was not an easy
idea to accept, particularly since Captain Williams had been assuring me all along that we
were going to win. I nodded my head and told
them I could take it. But I didn't know for a fact
that I wouldn't keel over when I heard the sentence or else go into hysterics and have to be
carried out. In the first place, it crossed my mind
that the Marines might just take me out and
shoot me before I could file an appeal. Greater
fuck-ups had occurred. Then, too, Denny had
said "in the long run." Just how long *was* "the
long run"? The "short run" had been almost five
months of solitary confinement, the brig, and
armed guards. I had already served six weeks

beyond my enlistment. I wanted out of the goddamn Marine Corps, and I had counted on being
discharged and back in Oklahoma within three
weeks. Now they were telling me I'd be out "in
the long run."

"You ready to get some chow?" Denny
asked.

I nodded, but I wasn't sure I was hungry.

One thing about the Marine Corps—it's like a
huge fraternity. If you stay in it for very long
you get to know a lot of the brothers, just from
being jerked around from one post to another.
And that's particularly true of the officer corps.
So Blue had plenty of friends in Vietnam, and it
didn't take him long to go through the First
Marine duty roster and find someone in headquarters he'd known at Annapolis or Quantico
or here in Vietnam.

He may have spent half the afternoon to set
it all up, but by that evening he was on his way,
and the next morning he'd had spectacular results. Gene and Denny told me about it before
the trial, as we sat around in Captain Williams's
office and drank coffee from paper cups.

"He came into the barracks about six this
morning. Said he'd been out on patrol all night.
Went to Son Trang 4. Paced everything off. Made
notes. We've got the whole picture—the position
of the huts, the dimensions of the area, distances
from the huts to the jungle. We know more at
this point than the prosecution."

Gene reached in his pocket, pulled out a
folded yellow sheet from a legal pad, and
handed it to me.

"Here. He drew this map for us. See if it jibes with your recollections."

I unfolded the sheet and stared at the precise drawings and figures, with arrows indicating directions. For a second or two it was meaningless. Then it began to make sense.

"Yeah," I said. "This is the place. We came up this path and heard men's voices coming out of one of these huts. Here's the first one we entered. And over here is the clearing. But I didn't realize the woods were so close to where the women were standing. They could have heard somebody whispering signals to them. That explains how they knew when to duck and run. It all looked slightly larger in the dark."

Denny shook his head in wonder.

"Did you know Ollie went out on a combat patrol last night just to get that information for us?"

I nodded as I studied the map, remembering that night, watching it take shape again between the tiny squares labeled "huts" and the dark pencil whorls labeled "woods."

"It doesn't surprise me," I mumbled.

"But that was pretty dangerous, don't you think?"

"It depends on who he went out with and who saw him go," I said. "If they find out about it back at headquarters, it might be his ass."

"I'm talking about the Vietcong," said Denny, obviously annoyed with me.

"Look," I said, "he wasn't in any danger of getting killed, if that's what you mean. The Vietcong couldn't kill him. Courting danger, he was in his element. He loved every minute of it. I can guarantee you he's been dreaming about it every night back at Quantico, wondering if he'd ever get to do it again. I'm just afraid somebody will turn him in. Who took him out on patrol?"

Gene grinned.

"You'll never guess."

"Lieutenant Ambort," I said.

"You're way off," he said.

I guessed two or three other guys, but Gene said I was still way off. Then he told me.

"It was your old buddy Lieutenant Lloyd Grant."

I was stunned. I couldn't believe North had been so dumb. Grant was a by-the-numbers bastard, the 90-day-wonder whose report had gotten us all into trouble in the first place. As a matter of fact, he was a witness for the prosecution.

"I'm not sure which of them surprises me more—North for trusting Grant or Grant for taking North out with him. Are you sure it was worth the risk just to get this map?"

"But you haven't heard it all," said Denny. "Ollie had a long talk with Grant. He's been in combat for the last four months. He's an entirely different Marine. The prosecution may be surprised when he gets on the stand."

"You mean he's going to take back what he said in his report?" I asked, still skeptical.

"No, he can't do that," said Denny patiently. "But how he tells the story can make all the difference in the world. Also, it will be important how he answers on cross-examination. He may end up being more helpful to us than to them."

I nodded, but none of it really made sense. I figured our only hope had been to sneak out there and gather evidence without tipping our hand. Now everyone on the prosecutor's staff would know what we'd learned and how we learned it. And all we had for our efforts were a few chicken scratches on a piece of yellow paper.

"Ollie came up with something else as well," said Gene, apparently reading my mind. "The village was known among the Vietnamese themselves as a Cong hideout. Still is. In fact, Ollie found out that there are active chapters of two communist organizations there—the Farmers Association and the Mothers and Sisters Association. The Mothers and Sisters Association is a bunch of women trained for sabotage and murder. We figure you must have run into some Mothers and Sisters that night."

"So they may have been armed themselves?"

"It's a distinct possibility," said Gene.

"What about the bodies? Did Lieutenant North find out what kind of bullets killed those people?"

"No," said Gene. "But he found out something almost as good. They were buried two days later right there in the village. The Marines could have sent in some ballistics experts 24 hours after the incident to confirm or refute your story. *They didn't.*"

"That's pretty good, isn't it?" I said, brightening up.

"It's great," said Gene.

Then something occurred to me.

"But it will be more useful on appeal than during the actual trial, right?"

"Right," Gene said. "But it will be helpful during the trial too. This man North has brought us a long way down the road in a few hours. At this rate we'll make it hard for that jury to convict you, though in the end they will."

"By the way," Denny added, "do you know a Sergeant Meyer?"

"Sure," I said. "A little dark guy with a mustache. He's a good man."

"Well, he's the first witness for the prosecution. But don't worry about that. North talked to him too."

The morning was taken up with motions for dismissal and change of venue (all denied) and by opening statements. For the first time I had an opportunity to size up the prosecutor. His name was Robert Brown, and he was a Marine Corps captain. About thirty years old, he had short-cropped brown hair and dark eyes. Throughout the trial he was thorough and methodical in the way he presented his case, and it was only in his closing statement that I discovered some emotion smoldering beneath that carefully controlled exterior. The impression I had that first day was of a man who had grown up with a law book in his hand.

I remember mentioning this to Gene, who replied, "There's an old saying that when you have the law on your side, you pound on the law; and when you don't have the law, you pound on the table. He thinks the law is on his side right now. That's why he's so smooth and unemotional. By the end of this trial, we'll have him pounding on the table."

Sure enough, we did. But on that first morning, he was all facts, as if the outcome of the trial were self-evident. He told how we had gone out into the field with orders to exact revenge for the death of Sergeant Lyons. (True.) How we'd come upon the small village of Son Trang 4. (True.) How we'd found nothing but women and children there. (True.) How we'd herded them all out into a clearing in the woods. (True.) And how, without the slightest provocation, we had shot them down, killing sixteen. (Half-true.) Indeed, except for Brown's assertion that we were not provoked in any way, I had no quarrel with his summary of the case, and I was a little disturbed that he could find in those same facts sufficient reason to try me for 16 counts of murder.

Then Captain Williams made the opening statement for our side, and he adopted the same matter-of-fact style, walking up and down in front of the jury, his tall frame occasionally bending in the middle as he leaned forward to stress a point. He spent a great deal of time on the question of our motivation, emphasizing the fact that it was night, that a number of men had already been killed in that area, and that we were under heavy pressure. He gave our account of the few seconds during which we had shot and killed the 16 civilians, and then he pointed out what he called "procedural errors" in the investigation that followed. Among these, he mentioned the failure to perform autopsies on the corpses, despite the fact that they weren't buried for two days. So Lieutenant North's intelligence paid off in the first day of the trial.

When Lieutenant Williams finished, the judge advocate glanced at his watch and called a recess until after lunch. We plowed through the swarm of reporters (larger now than at 9:00 when we entered) and made our way back to the captain's cubicle, which everyone was now calling "headquarters."

Lieutenant North was waiting there for us, clear-eyed and fresh, though he couldn't have had more than four hours sleep.

"How did it go?" he asked, as he rose from the wooden chair.

"Great," said Gene. "The captain here was flawless."

"How are you holding up?" Lieutenant North said to me. "You look a little hot."

I grinned. My utilities were so wet they were sticking to my skin, and my face must have been bright red. Denny and Gene were soaked too, and only Captain Williams seemed relatively untouched, with no more than a few beads of perspiration dotting his high forehead. Dick and Harry had been the lucky ones. They'd stayed in the cubicle all day, reading law books in a room where the temperature wasn't more than 95 degrees; then they'd headed down the hill.

"I hear you did a little reconnoitering," I said. "How did it go?"

North grinned and lit up a cigar as we all settled into chairs.

"It was great to be back," he said, and I knew how he must have felt.

"Now what do we need to know?" he asked Denny.

"We would like to locate that rifle, or at least the records. You know better than we do how unusual it is to misplace a weapon or ordnance records pertaining to a weapon. We think somebody knows where to put his hands on both."

Lieutenant North made an ashtray out of his cupped hand and flicked his cigar.

"I guess we should begin with the Marine who was carrying the rifle. Is he still around so we can talk to him?"

"He's certainly not going anywhere," said Denny. "He's serving twelve consecutive life sentences for the same incident Randy's being tried for. But he doesn't know what happened to his rifle. He turned it in to ordnance and that's the last he ever saw of it."

"Then I'll start someplace else," said Lieutenant North, and popped to his feet.

"I've already talked to ordnance," said Denny. "But you're welcome to try yourself."

"I think I know what may have happened," said North. "I'm going to try another avenue."

He winked at me and was gone in a cloud of cigar smoke.

I was glad he was going to tackle the problem. I knew that if the rifle or the records still existed, he would find them. And if he didn't find them, then I would know they had been destroyed.

"Where do you suppose he's off to?" Gene asked.

"Somewhere he's not supposed to go," said Captain Williams with a smile.

"Why do you say that?" said Gene.

"Because," said Captain Williams, "that's the only place he'll find what he's looking for."

That afternoon the prosecution began to present its witnesses, and the first of these was a U.S. Marine, my old buddy Sergeant Meyer.

When the sergeant-at-arms called Meyer's name I turned around to watch him walk down the aisle, looking trim and tanned. I knew he was there under duress, and I just wanted to give him a signal, so he wouldn't think I held it against him. I knew if given half a chance, he would try to help me. I remembered that Lieutenant North had talked to him and wondered what Meyer had said.

As he walked past me, I saw his eyes cut in my direction. Then, with arms rigid by his side, he lifted the palm of his left hand and sliced the air once—the only wave he could risk. I relaxed. Everything was okay between us.

After Meyer was sworn in, Captain Brown rose and began to question him.

"Sergeant Meyer, were you present on the night of March 2 when a patrol led by Lance Corporal Randy Herrod returned from the bush?"

"I was," said Meyer.

"Would you please tell us what happened."

Meyer briefly recited the events of that evening, with Brown interrupting him from time to time to ask clarifying questions.

"You say Lance Corporal Herrod said he had 'gotten some.' I take it you mean he had killed some people. Is that right?"

"Yes, sir."

"And did he say 'Vietcong' or 'enemy'?"

"No, sir."

"Just 'some,' is that right?"

"Yes, sir."

What Brown clearly wanted Meyer to say was that I had lied about how many people we had killed and who they were. In a way, of course, I *had* lied. After all, when Meyer had asked me if we had killed any of the enemy that night, I had said we had "gotten some," knowing

that he would assume I was talking about Vietcong guerrillas, not civilian women and children. Brown knew the whole story and went
after it with a vengeance. I'll say this, however:
Meyer didn't just blurt out what I'd said. He
made Brown work to get the words.

When Brown was finished with his questioning, the story of my "lying" was out in the
open for the jury to consider. I had been deliberately evasive in my report of the action. Clearly
I'd been trying to cover up something. My be-
havior seriously undermined my credibility. I
couldn't quarrel with either the facts or with the
logic of that conclusion.

Then it was our turn, and for the first time
Gene stood up and took over the defense.

"Sergeant, let's forget, for the moment,
about hearsay evidence. Let's talk about what
you saw and heard that night as opposed to what
somebody else told you. But first, let me ask you
this: Do you think from a distance of, say, two or
three miles you could distinguish between different kinds of gunfire?"

"Maybe," said Meyer. "It would depend."

"Let me be more specific," Gene said. "Could
you tell the difference between rifle fire and machine gun fire or rifle fire and M-79 fire?"

"Oh, sure," said Meyer.

"Good. Now, on that same night of March 2,
did you hear any gunfire in the distance?"

"Yes," Meyer said emphatically. "I heard firing in the vicinity of Son Trang 4."

"Would you describe what you heard?"

"Yes, sir," said Meyer. "I heard Vietcong machine gun fire followed immediately by our rifle
fire."

Captain Brown half rose in his seat and had his mouth open to speak, but Gene beat him to it.

"You say you heard Vietcong fire. How did you know it wasn't your team's machine gun firing at the Vietcong?" asked Gene.

"Because Herrod's team didn't have a machine gun with them," Meyer said. "Besides, we captured the gun four days later. The Cong had salvaged it from a downed helicopter. It's got to have been the one they used in that ambush."

This time Captain Brown was on his feet with an objection.

"Sustained," said the judge advocate. "The jury will disregard that remark. Try not to draw conclusions, Sergeant."

I figured we'd lost that round, but Gene went back to the same point in his next question.

"And how long after the machine gun did you hear the grenade launcher and rifle fire?"

"About 30 seconds," Meyer said.

My heart sank just a little. It was too long a delay, and I wondered if the jury sensed that. We had fired almost simultaneously, getting off a burst within a second or two after the first flash of flame. If we'd waited 30 seconds we'd have been shipped back home in body bags. I wished Meyer had said five seconds, but he was trying to help us out as much as he could.

Gene, who didn't understand the problem with Meyer's reply, nevertheless concentrated on the existence of the machine gun fire rather than how quickly we had followed up with a response. He was even able to reintroduce the captured weapon into the testimony.

"Tell me, Sergeant," he said, "do the Vietcong ever use weapons like machine guns?"

"Yes, sir, they do," said Meyer.

"American machine guns?"

"Yes, sir."

"And how do they get them?" Gene asked.

Meyer broke into a grin.

"They capture them."

"Was there any indication they might have been using captured machine guns near Son Trang 4 around that time?"

By then Captain Brown was grinning, but he didn't object.

"Yes, sir," said Meyer. "Only four days later, right there at Son Trang 4, we recovered a machine gun the Cong had captured from a downed helicopter."

"Thank you, Sergeant," Gene said. "That's all I have for this witness."

Next morning I sat in my seat, watching the flies zigzagging through the air, and tried to be objective about how Meyer had come across. He had been their witness, but on balance his testimony had been more useful to us—or so I concluded, even after trying to think like a lawyer and see both sides.

Of course there was the nagging question of why I had lied, and I wasn't sure of the answer myself. I hoped I could explain myself in terms of a desire to tell Lieutenant Ambort what he wanted to hear, but I really couldn't say whether or not that was the entire reason. Maybe I'd actually been afraid someone would accuse us of slaughtering civilians. The others had raised that possibility as we were coming back that night.

Did their fears affect me? I honestly didn't think so, but I had my doubts that I could convince the jury.

"Call your next witness," said the judge advocate to Captain Brown.

"The prosecution calls Lieutenant Lloyd Grant."

"Lieutenant Lloyd Grant!" shouted the sergeant-at-arms, as if Lieutenant Grant were down in the barracks at the foot of the hill.

Now, I thought, we would be hearing the gory part. I had not seen what we left behind, the people sprawled there on the ground, dead or dying. I had tried not to think about them. They were irrevocably gone now, tiny women and tinier children, lost forever in a flash of light and flying metal. I knew that what we had done was done in fear, and I knew if I found myself in the same situation, I would do it all over again. Or I hoped I would, since—like those women and children—I too wanted to live.

But I didn't want to hear about it, particularly not from Lloyd Grant, whose vivid report —written in the white heat of anger—I still remembered.

As Lieutenant Grant walked toward the witness chair I had my first opportunity to see him. He was trim but muscular, perhaps in his middle twenties, a man I would have passed without noticing on the street. But there was something about him that was distinctive—the way he talked. He was from Connecticut and spoke with what seemed to me a heavy accent, though I suppose he would have thought the same of me.

Captain Brown got down to business immediately.

"Lieutenant Grant," he said, "would you please tell us what you found when you arrived at Son Trang 4 on the morning of May 3."

Grant nodded.

"We were led to a small village by a woman, who wanted to show us something. When we got there we saw a number of bodies lying on the ground. Women and children. We checked to see if anyone was alive, but all were dead. There were sixteen. Some of the women from the nearby village came toward us, hesitantly. We had an interpreter with us, so we asked them what had happened. They told us that an American patrol had come through the village in the middle of the night, and that later they had heard shooting. They said when they came out at daybreak, they found the dead bodies."

"Would you describe the condition of the bodies?" said Captain Brown. "I mean, how had these people died?"

"They seemed to have all died from gunshot or shrapnel wounds. We couldn't really be sure. Since we had no medical personnel with us, we didn't investigate further."

"What was your reaction at the time?" Captain Brown asked.

I glanced over at Captain Williams and Gene, expecting an objection; but they made none.

"I was upset. We all were. It wasn't a particularly pleasant sight."

I was beginning to sense something odd in Grant's answers, a clipped reticent quality. He wasn't volunteering anything. Captain Brown was having to fish for answers, and what he was getting was not what he wanted. He had begun to frown. He went over and over the same ground for what seemed hours. Then we broke for lunch, and when court reconvened he started out in a slightly different vein.

"Lieutenant Grant," he said, "I have here a report you wrote about this incident. Do you remember such a report?"

"Yes, sir, I do," Grant said.

"If you will permit me, let me read a few paragraphs from your earlier account of what you found there."

Grant sat without expression while Captain Brown read from the report, which was full of angry phrases like "brutal slaughter" and "unconscionable waste of life." After Captain Brown had read a few paragraphs, he stopped and looked at Lieutenant Grant.

"Is that what you wrote, Lieutenant?"

"Yes, sir, it is."

Captain Brown started to ask another question, then changed his mind.

"That's all. Thank you, Lieutenant."

So in his testimony, Lieutenant Grant had repeated the facts of his report, though not in the same language he had used earlier. This time he had been matter-of-fact, all business—a very competent witness, but not an emotional one.

When Captain Brown had finished, Gene rose for cross-examination.

"Lieutenant Grant," he said, "when you made that discovery at Son Trang 4, were you there as a combat officer?"

"No sir. I was an intelligence officer at the time."

"New to Vietnam?"

Lieutenant Grant nodded.

"I had been here only two or three weeks."

Gene nodded, adopting a sympathetic tone in his questioning.

"Up till that time had you ever been in combat?"

Grant said that he had not.

"And what are your duties now?" Gene asked.

"I command a combat platoon."

"Have you seen much combat, Lieutenant?"

Lieutenant Grant smiled grimly.

"A lot."

"Tell me something, Lieutenant," Gene said. "What instructions do you give your men when they encounter suspicious movement in the field?"

Grant leaned forward for emphasis.

"I tell them that if they have the slightest indication there's danger, to fire first and ask questions later."

"And what do you tell them about night fighting?"

"I tell them anything moving is fair game."

Gene questioned him about the dangers of combat in this region, and Grant said the right things. To my right, Captain Brown was frowning again, but Gene kept at it for the rest of the afternoon. Captain Brown must have figured somebody had gotten to his witnesses, but he clearly didn't know who it was. The civilians were hemmed in by red tape, and I was under constant guard. Captain Williams had spent all his time around the Judge Advocate's Office, holding court for the rest of us. So who had talked to Meyer and Grant, stationed at a combat outpost? Brown didn't know the answer to that question, and it was clearly bothering him.

I must admit I enjoyed his frustration, particularly knowing that North was somewhere at this very moment, digging up new information to undermine the prosecution's case; and as we recessed that afternoon, I wondered where he was and what he was up to. Because of him things were beginning to swing our way. I wondered how long he had talked to Lieutenant Grant and to what extent he had influenced Grant's testimony. After thinking it over, I finally concluded that Grant had changed his mind because of what had happened to him over the last several months rather than because of what North had said, but from Gene's confidence in asking Grant questions about his recent experience in combat, it was clear that North had fed Gene most of his lines for today's cross-examination. As Gene had told me, you don't ask a hostile witness questions to which you don't already know the answers.

That night I got to bed very early and fell asleep as soon as my head hit the pillow. The worst of the prosecution's witnesses had come and gone with Lieutenant Grant. Meyer had clearly helped. And North was on the loose, breaking into the ordnance files of the Marine Corps—or so I hoped. I wasn't home free—and Gene and Denny were still sticking by their prediction of a win on appeal—but I had concluded that if I had to, I could take whatever delay an appeal would bring.

The next morning I woke up early; and after lying in bed for a few minutes, I decided to get

up and get out into the air while it was still cool
—though at 6:30 A.M. the temperature was probably already pushing 90 degrees.

After I'd dressed and shaved, I called Rodriguez, my chaser for the day, and told him to pick
me up early so I'd have at least a half hour to
relax before meeting Gene, Denny, and the others over at Captain Williams's office. As we were
crossing the street, I glanced down the steep hill
and saw something on the side of the road that
caught my attention. It was a man on all fours,
crawling, and for a moment I thought he was
hurt—maybe a hit-and-run victim.

Then, as I watched, I saw the glint of the
aluminum crutches; and I realized who it was.
Rodriguez had stopped on the curb and was following my gaze.

"Hey!" he yelled. "Look at that!"

I stood there for a moment, trying to figure
out what to do. It was Dick Miller, and he was
making his way up the hill by dragging himself a
few feet at a time. I had seen him move quickly
and easily on level ground; but the climb up this
hill was practically vertical, and it was even
tough on Gene, Denny, and the others. For Dick
it was impossible, so he had to crawl, pulling the
dead weight of his legs behind him.

I thought about his sacrifices in coming all
the way over here, and I added on to those the
humiliation of having to make that crawl every
morning. Before he arrived in Vietnam he
hadn't known who I was, yet he came anyway.
For a few seconds I had a hard time swallowing.

"Maybe we can give him some help," Rodriguez said.

"No," I said. "Leave him alone. He doesn't need any help."

"You know the guy?"

"Yeah," I said. "I know him. He's on my defense team."

"What's wrong with him?"

"He's crippled."

"The poor bastard."

"Yeah," I said. "Let's go inside so he won't see us staring at him."

(Years later I read in an Arkansas newspaper that Dick Miller had killed himself. It seems that on top of everything else, he'd gotten cancer. I called Gene, and we both said he must have been worried about how he would pay the bills, or the effect his illness might have on his family; because, remembering him crawling up that steep hillside in Vietnam, neither one of us could believe Dick wasn't able to take whatever cancer had to offer.)

After court convened, the prosecution called Lieutenant Ambort to the stand. I wasn't worried about his testimony too much, because I knew he was going to do what he could to take the heat off of me. What did worry me was what he might say inadvertently about the way we fought the war at LZ Ross. He knew a little too much about the numbers and kinds of weapons I took into the bush, and he could also tell some out-of-school tales about the "killer teams" and the exotic ways we dreamed up to kill the enemy. I didn't think he would volunteer such information, but I wasn't positive.

"Lieutenant Ambort," said Captain Brown,

"you were the defendant's company commander, weren't you?"

"For the last couple of months he was at LZ Ross, yes, sir."

"And it was you who ordered him on the patrol where these sixteen women and children were killed, is that right?"

"That's right, sir," said Lieutenant Ambort.

"Would you tell the court what you told the defendant just before he led his patrol into the bush on the night of March 3."

Lieutenant Ambort answered in a matter-of-fact voice.

"I told them that a lot of men had been killed recently, that there were Vietcong crawling all over the countryside, and that they were to shoot first and ask questions later."

"Do you remember saying anything about a Sergeant Lyons as you were giving Lance Corporal Herrod his orders?"

"I believe I told him to tell his men that this patrol was dedicated to Sergeant Lyons, who had been killed earlier in the day—in an ambush."

"Did you in any way suggest to them that they avenge the death of Sergeant Lyons?"

Lieutenant Ambort hesitated for a moment. In his answers, he had been trying to take some of the blame off my shoulders, but he suddenly realized where Brown was leading him. The fact that he had told me to bring back a few scalps made me look worse, not better.

"I may have said something like that," Lieutenant Ambort finally replied.

"Did you tell him to 'get some' for Sergeant Lyons?"

"It's possible I said something like that," said Lieutenant Ambort. "But you say things like that all the time. You have to keep the men psyched up. It's hard to get them to go back into the bush day after day, particularly when you've just lost fifteen or twenty men."

Captain Brown held up his hand.

"That's all right, Lieutenant. I understand. Now tell me what happened when Lance Corporal Herrod and the others came in the next morning. Did you see them when they hit camp?"

"Yes," he said. "Herrod came to my tent."

"What did he say?"

"He told me they'd been ambushed, been fired at."

"Did he tell you anything about who ambushed them, how many there were, how many they'd killed?"

"He said they'd killed some. He didn't know how many."

"Did he say they were men? Vietcong?"

"He didn't say. I don't think he knew."

"Did he try to make you believe he'd killed Vietcong fighters?"

"I don't recall that he did or didn't."

Captain Brown was unhappy, and I could see the muscles in his jaw ripple as he clenched his teeth. But he remained poised and quiet-spoken. He knew he would have to be a little more aggressive in dealing with Lieutenant Ambort, who was clearly hostile. Again I had the feeling that we were doing very well with his witnesses.

"Lieutenant Ambort, when you wrote up the report of this incident, did you give an accurate account of what happened?"

Without hesitation Lieutenant Ambort replied, "No, sir, I did not."

"In what way was your account inaccurate?" asked Captain Brown.

"I reported that the patrol had captured an enemy weapon."

"And they had not done so?"

"They had not."

"In other words, you lied on that report?"

"Yes," said Lieutenant Ambort.

"And can you tell this court why you lied?"

Lieutenant Ambort nodded.

"Yes, sir," he said. "I had heard about Lieutenant Grant's report the next day, and I knew it would look pretty bad for the patrol. I thought it might lend credibility to their story if a weapon had been found. So I supplied a weapon. It was a stupid thing for me to do, but later the machine gun *was* found."

Captain Brown hesitated, then ignored the remark; but it had angered him.

"Weren't you later reprimanded for that lie?" he said, eyes glinting.

"Yes, sir," Lieutenant Ambort said.

"And what was your punishment?" asked Captain Brown.

"I was fined $500."

Having pressed that point home by way of punishment, Captain Brown went back over the same incidents, trying to get Lieutenant Ambort to admit that I had lied outright about the people we'd killed, that I had said they were Vietcong guerrillas. But he got nowhere. Lieutenant Ambort dug in and held his ground, in part, I suspected, because Captain Brown had rubbed his nose in the reprimand. Finally Brown gave up and turned the witness over to the defense.

In cross-examination Lieutenant Ambort said we had reacted the way we'd been trained to react, that he would have done the same thing under similar circumstances.

So we had fared extremely well with the first three witnesses, turning them to our own advantage. Everyone was pleased with where we stood at the end of this latest round. As Denny cleared off the table, Gene asked Harry what he thought.

"We're in great shape," he said. "Another day or two like this and there's not an appeals court in the country that won't throw this out. So far they have no case."

Gene nodded and began to move toward the door, stopping to let Captain Brown pass in front of him, smiling cordially as he did so.

Then, when Brown was out of earshot, he said to Harry, "If we're still this far ahead after the Vietnamese women tomorrow, I'd say we're home free."

I liked the sound of "home free," even if he didn't mean it literally, and I was also pleased to hear that his assessment of the trial coincided with mine. Maybe it meant I was beginning to think like a lawyer.

As we left the courtroom the reporters crowded around, first asking us questions in ordinary voices, then as we passed through the crowd, shouting at our backs. It was hard not to stop and talk to them, particularly the ones from Oklahoma, but Gene reminded me to smile and keep moving. They trailed across the street after us, still bombarding us. However, when we entered the Quonset hut that served as the judge advocate's building, they knew better than to follow.

Dick and Harry started down the hill, as they did every night; and Gene, Denny, Captain Williams, and I went to headquarters for a drink of bourbon and a recap of the day's proceedings. I had hoped Lieutenant North would be waiting for us, but when we got there, the cubicle was empty.

"Where do you suppose Ollie North is?" Denny asked, directing his question to nobody in particular.

"I'd guess he spent the day at Division headquarters," said Captain Williams. "That's where all the incriminating paperwork is buried."

"I'd guess he was back at LZ Ross," I said, "talking to some of the guys there and waiting till dark."

"Why waiting until dark?" Denny asked.

"So he can go out with another killer team," I said.

The others thought it was a big joke, but I was dead serious, as they were soon to find out.

Next came the Vietnamese women, who, we learned, had been reluctant to testify and had been paid $6 for appearing at this trial, as at the earlier ones. Old, shriveled, dressed in their pajama-like rags, they looked like two corn shuck dolls, each in her turn trudging up to the witness chair.

The first, a Mrs. Thiem, told the same story she had told at the other trials. She had seen us enter the village and had gone to hide. Later she had heard the shots. That was all.

But armed with what he had learned from Lieutenant North's reconnoiter, Gene was able to score valuable points on his cross-examination.

"What were the political sympathies of the people in that hamlet?"

Through an interpreter Mrs. Thiem told the truth. She said they were mostly Vietcong.

"What organizations do people there belong to?"

Her answer: the Mothers and Sisters Association, the Farmers Association. She added that her daughter, who had been among the 16 killed, had been spending the night with a man who was a Vietcong.

The second woman, 70-year-old Mrs. Thiphuong, told essentially the same story that Mrs. Thiem told. On cross-examination, she said that the Cong dominated the village, and that they had carried her son away several months earlier.

So we had established a couple of important facts that none of the earlier defense attorneys brought out: 1) the Vietcong ran the village, and 2) the Cong men had been there that night, because Mrs. Thiem's daughter had been with one of them.

Meanwhile, Denny had talked to Lieutenant North about another project.

"It would be important in an appeal to know just how heavily the opinion is stacked against us. You're an officer and have access to the Officers' Club. Nobody knows who you are. Do you suppose you could run a quiet poll of about 50 officers and see if they expect Herrod to be convicted or acquitted? No need to have their names. What we really want is a count."

"What results do you expect?" Lieutenant North asked.

"In the few interviews that I've conducted, I believe you're going to encounter a strong sentiment for conviction. And if I'm right, then such a poll will lend credibility to our request for a change of venue and a new trial."

So North went to work.

Curiously, this mission turned out to be more dangerous than the previous one. He went into the Officers' Club that night and began to move around, quietly asking each officer present what he or she thought the outcome of the trial would be. Without exception they said I'd be convicted, that I was as guilty as sin.

Though he conducted his survey as discreetly as possible, suddenly Lieutenant North found himself confronted by a major, who was slightly drunk and ready for a fight.

"What the hell are you up to, going around asking questions about that trial?"

Lieutenant North tried to brush the major aside, but the man started cursing and screaming, so the lieutenant retreated through the door, probably for the first time in his life backing away from a fight, doing so in the interest of my defense. The major didn't know how lucky he'd been, given North's boxing experience and his love of mixing it up.

When he came in the next morning, North reported 39 out of 40 had voted for conviction, and one had wanted to fight.

Denny seemed pleased. Clearly an appeal on

those grounds had merit. We had laid one more
brick in what was becoming a solid case for the
appellate court.

Meanwhile, though Garrison was making progress in his investigation, one question kept
haunting him: "Where was the rifle that
Schwartz had been carrying, the M-16 with the
shattered stock?" An inquiry by Lieutenant
Ambort had revealed that the weapon had been
returned to ordnance for repair. But there it had
disappeared, despite the fact that all military
weapons are carefully accounted for by serial
number, and that the Corps regards it as a serious matter if one is ever lost. Yet they were telling us they didn't know where this particular
weapon was.

Garrison and North were to search for that
rifle for the rest of the trial, but no one at any
level of command would give them an indication of where it was or why it had disappeared.
An expert examination of the stock was all we
needed to prove that the enemy had fired on us.
Somebody obviously knew that.

Realizing that something was afoot, Lieutenant North began to make inquiries. After a
couple of days he reported back to Gene and
Captain Williams that there was correspondence
between General Edwin Wheeler and the Pentagon to the effect that I was to be convicted—
whatever. Somehow Lieutenant North had gotten good information, and with a couple of calls
to Washington, giving the precise date and the
signatures involved, we obtained "stipulations"
from the Marine Corps that such documents did
indeed exist and that they contained evidence

prejudicial to my case. Again, good ammunition for an appeal.

When Boyd took the stand I felt sorry for him. He was shattered emotionally, scared to death, and close to tears. He blurted out his story, looking at me as if I were going to jump him at any moment. At this point I didn't care what he was saying. I figured he'd done what he had to.

He managed to get it all out without breaking down, but he had to pass right in front of me on the way out. Somehow I couldn't let him leave the courtroom without letting him know I didn't blame him, so I stood up and offered him my hand. He hesitated, shook hands quickly, and then burst into tears and stumbled out of the room. I wasn't sure how the court would take this, so I sat down quickly and said nothing. And the trial continued.

Meanwhile, Lieutenant North had nothing to do; and since he wasn't supposed to testify for several more days, he disappeared. No one missed him for a while. Then at noon break one day I came into the lawyers' office and saw Gene, Denny, and Captain Williams with worried faces.

"What's the matter?" I asked.

"It's Lieutenant North," said Gene. "He's about to get himself killed."

"What do you mean?" I asked. I couldn't believe it.

"The damn fool is going out on combat missions," said Denny. "Night before last he went out on an all-night patrol. Last night he went with a medevac unit to remove the wounded from an area under attack. They were fired on. People were getting killed."

"He's just that way," I said. "Don't worry. He won't get killed."

"If he does," said Gene, "I hope he waits till he testifies. Can't you order him to stop it, Captain?"

"I can," said Captain Williams. "But somehow I don't think I will. Would you?"

"No," said Gene. "I don't guess I would."

A VERDICT

WE HAD ALREADY agreed that I would take the stand in my own defense, and for a while I was looking forward to the moment when I could tell my own story. When the time came, however, I began to feel my stomach churning; and when I walked the few steps to the witness stand I was a little shaky. Gene gave me a reassuring nod, and I managed to settle into the chair without appearing too nervous. I felt the sweat begin to form on my forehead, and above me the fan blade was a blur in the still air.

After Gene had asked me a few preliminary questions about my background and how I had come to be in Vietnam, he said in a quiet voice, "All right, Randy, now I want you to tell us exactly what happened that night on patrol. Take your time. Try to remember everything. Just the way it happened."

I knew he was going to ask the question, but we hadn't rehearsed this testimony.

"But before you begin," he said, "with the court's permission I'm going to set up a map so we can all follow the story as he tells it."

The map, mounted on a tripod, was a blown-up version of the one Lieutenant North had made when he had gone out on patrol. I realized that for the first time the court could see just how such an engagement had taken place, and I was encouraged by the thought.

"All right," he said. "Now tell us what happened in your own words."

I went through it all one more time—from the moment we got the orders to go out on patrol until I was placed under arrest. Of course Gene knew my version of what had happened; and as I told my story, he interrupted to ask me questions, reminding me to include everything in my account, all the details, down to the smallest snatch of conversation.

"What did Lieutenant Ambort say to you as you were about to leave?"

"What weapons were you carrying?"

"What kind of voices did you hear? How many different people could you distinguish?"

"How well could you see at that moment?"

"Where did the flashes come from?"

He hadn't forgotten a word I had told him. He had it all arranged in his mind, the entire picture, with each piece in its proper place. And when I left out something, he would make me go back and put it in. I realized that with Gene leading me through the testimony, I wouldn't make any bad mistakes; so for the first time since I had come into the courtroom, I felt my muscles begin to relax. I knew that the trial was almost over and that whatever happened, I would have told my side of the story and told it right. By the time I had finished, I had explained the full complexity of our situation that night, and I was satisfied that anyone who had been in combat would understand what we had done.

"Your witness, Captain," he said, and gave me a nod as he sat down.

Gene and Denny had warned me that Captain Brown would have to tear into my testimony in order to compensate for the failure of his own witnesses, so I was fully prepared for the intensity of what followed. I just wasn't anticipating the amount of time I would be on the witness stand: somewhere between eleven and twelve hours, mostly answering the same old questions over and over again.

"Corporal Herrod," he began, "you lied to your company commander when you first came off patrol, didn't you?"

"Yes, sir," I said.

His tone was neutral, but I could see the hard look in his eye. He would not be easy on me.

"Why did you tell a deliberate lie?"

"Because I knew Lieutenant Ambort was hoping we would get some of the Vietcong. The ones who had killed Sergeant Lyons. So I told him what he wanted to hear."

"Are you sure you didn't lie for another reason? Isn't it true that you lied because you knew you and your men had committed an act of cold-blooded murder, an act you hoped you could cover up?"

"No, sir," I answered as calmly as I could. "It never occurred to me that we hadn't acted in self-defense."

He looked surprised.

"It never occurred to you that gunning down sixteen civilian women and children wasn't a crime?"

"Sir, we were fired on first," I said.

"By unarmed noncombatants?"

"By someone."

"All right, Corporal," he said. "Tell me again just how it happened that night."

I told the story again, remembering every detail I could. I figured that if I simply stuck to the truth, in the end whatever I said would be consistent.

When I finished, he smiled and shook his head in disbelief.

"Isn't it true that you lied to Lieutenant Ambort because you thought the artillery fire he called in would clean up your mess for you? Didn't you expect those bodies to be blown to bits? Then you would have been home free, wouldn't you?"

"No, sir. I can honestly say that I never thought about the artillery. Like I said before, I simply wanted to tell Lieutenant Ambort something that would cheer him up. It was a mistake. I wish now I'd told the truth."

"I'll bet you do," he said, his voice heavy with irony.

I remember thinking that I had said all there was to say on the subject, but Captain Brown kept coming back to the same point again and again.

"Why did you lie, Corporal Herrod?"

I know he asked that question fifteen or twenty times, and in a variety of ways. I finally realized that he wasn't trying to break me down or even to catch me in an inconsistency. He was emphasizing and reemphasizing the same point to the jury: that I had lied to Lieutenant Ambort from the beginning, and that I might well be lying now.

Every time he asked the question, however, I answered calmly and with courtesy. I knew that if I lost my temper or seemed undisciplined, the officers facing me might begin to believe the picture he was trying to paint—that of a man capable of wildly impulsive and irresponsible acts.

The more I maintained my composure, the more persistent he became. If he couldn't get me to lose my cool, then he would wear me down—minute by minute, hour by hour. He must have asked me thirty times to retell the story of the ambush, probing for inconsistencies, pretending to misunderstand me in order to trip me up. He asked the same question ten different ways, and still I gave him the same answers.

At times he would pretend to be friendly. At other times he would become openly hostile and abusive. But mostly he was cold and clinical—and I tried to be the same way. I also made it a point to respond to the most hostile questioning with continuing courtesy. All the jury had been in combat. All of them knew how important discipline was to a successful mission.

Each time I went through the narrative I said to myself, "This will be the last round. After this one, he'll give up. All I have to do is tell it right one more time."

But he knew precisely what he was doing, and each time, after leaving the subject, he would ask another question, then with a sigh and a shrug of his shoulders, say, "All right, Corporal, let's go through it again. And this time try to tell us what really happened."

When my first day on the stand ended, I went back to our headquarters and had a couple of drinks, then hit the sack early. I felt as if I had been chopping wood all day.

On the afternoon of my second day, the moment finally came when I was too numb to think clearly. Had I been lying, I'm sure I would have begun to forget what I had said previously or to make mistakes. Because I was telling the truth, however, I was able to tell the story again and again without really concentrating on the details. I wondered why the others in the courtroom didn't fall asleep, but they sat through the entire grilling without breaking their concentration—the jurors, my lawyers, the prosecution, the reporters. All of them seemed to hang on every word.

Then suddenly it was over. I was sitting there, expecting to be asked one more time to tell the court what had *really* happened that night, when Captain Brown stepped back, looked at me for a long moment, and then turned to the jury.

"I have no more questions for this witness."

Then he walked back over to his chair and eased into it, obviously exhausted.

At that moment I felt a sense of release that could not have been much greater had they declared me "not guilty" on the spot and turned me loose. For me it was all over. I had taken the worst Captain Brown had to offer, kept my head, and told the truth from beginning to end. As I walked back to my seat I felt a little giddy, and I grinned at Gene, who nodded.

Of course, I had no illusions that I had swayed the jury. But I knew that I hadn't dug my own grave, and I was reasonably certain that my testimony would work in my favor when it was reviewed by an appeals judge.

That evening we had a mild celebration back in Captain Williams's office. Everyone agreed that I had done an outstanding job, and I was proud of myself.

"Who's on tap tomorrow?" I asked.

"Lieutenant North," said Denny, "if he's still alive."

"Don't worry about that," I said, but all the same I worried a little. I knew more than my civilian lawyers just how important his testimony would be. I was reasonably sure that I had been credible, but the credibility of an enlisted man and the credibility of a career officer are two different things. North's endorsement of my character and my conduct under fire would be crucial. If for any reason he couldn't make it, then our case would be weakened.

"Where is he?" I asked.

Both Denny and Gene shrugged their shoulders, and Captain Williams just laughed. He understood North.

The next morning, when my chaser and I started up the hill, I was a little nervous. Then I saw North, standing in front of the building. It was going to be a good day after all.

"Were you up all night?" I asked as we drew near.

"I got a little sleep," he said, "but not much."

Then Gene and the others joined us, and we

went inside. As soon as the court was convened, Gene called North to the stand.

It's difficult to explain the impact he made on the people in that small courtroom. Many of them were combat veterans who had risked their own lives and who knew the real thing when they saw it. It was not only what he said and the way he said it; it was also the way he looked and even the way he sat. In starched camouflage utilities, back at a 90 degree angle to his lap, arms "at 90s," with his lifer haircut (high and tight), spit-shined boots, silver jump wings, Annapolis ring on his finger—he looked like the ultimate military hero, the man all of us would like to have been. Many Americans recognized the same quality in him when he testified before a congressional committee almost twenty years later; but only professional soldiers could have fully appreciated what he seemed to be that day to a room full of tired military men, fighting a war that nobody much believed in anymore.

Although a civilian, Gene sensed the atmosphere North's appearance had created and treated him with obvious deference.

"Would you identify yourself, please, Lieutenant."

North gave his name and current post.

Gene asked him what he was doing in Vietnam, and Lieutenant North replied that he had taken leave to come back and testify on my behalf.

"And how did you happen to know Randy Herrod?"

As North began talking, I remember telling myself: "That was years ago—way back in my childhood." Yet I realized at the same time that those days seemed more real to me than the courtroom or the people in it.

"In other words, you were Herrod's immediate superior officer," Gene said.

"I was his platoon leader for most of that time."

"Was there anything special about that platoon?"

"It was a first-class fighting unit," North said. "The best."

"Did it receive any special honors?"

North nodded.

"We were named honor platoon for the 3rd Marines."

"And Randy Herrod was a member of that platoon?"

"He was."

"What kind of Marine was he?"

"One of the best I had," Lieutenant North said forcefully.

"Let me be more specific," said Gene. "Did he obey orders?"

"Yes, sir," said Lieutenant North. "I can think of no occasion when he didn't carry out orders to the letter."

"And did he behave himself otherwise?"

"At all times. He never got out of line. He was never a troublemaker."

"And what about in combat?"

"In combat he was outstanding. He was disciplined and steady. He always fought by the book."

"Would you say he displayed courage under fire?"

"Yes, sir, I would," said North. "As a matter

of fact, I recommended him for the Navy Cross, because of his courage during one firefight."

"Would you tell us precisely what happened during that engagement?"

"Yes, sir. Our company had bivouacked on the side of a hill. It was night, and the North Vietnamese suddenly attacked and overran us. Several of our men had been hit, one of them our machine gunner. Herrod, though wounded, ran from one foxhole to the other under heavy fire in order to take over the machine gun. He began firing at the enemy. I was standing right behind him, and I could see that he was making a big difference. A short time later a rocket round hit nearby, and the concussion knocked me unconscious. I was lying on the ground, fully exposed to enemy fire. Herrod crawled out of his foxhole and shielded me with his own body while he fought off the enemy with his machine gun. They were within 20 feet of us. He stayed with me until I regained consciousness and then returned to his post and began firing again."

"How would you characterize what he did?" Gene asked.

"He saved my life," Lieutenant North said.

It was an important moment in the trial. The men on the jury knew he had come all the way back from Quantico just to appear at this trial. Now they knew why. In the long silence that followed, Gene allowed them to think about what North had said.

Then he took up another line of questioning.

"Do you believe that Randy Herrod can get a fair trial in this court?" Gene asked.

"I don't know," North said evenly.

"And why would you have any doubts?"

"Because I ran an informal poll among the officers here on the base and discovered that 39 out of 40 already thought he was guilty and expected him to be convicted."

No objection from Captain Brown. So it was there on the record, available to the appellate judge when we petitioned for a reversal.

Gene said he had no more questions, and Captain Brown did not choose to cross-examine.

When Lieutenant North left the stand, all eyes followed him. I watched the faces of the seven men on the court and began to think for the first time since the trial began that we might have a chance to win.

Lieutenant North, however, was not our last witness. The next man to take the stand was a surprise to the prosecution—and to me as well. He was a lance corporal from another outfit, a guy I had never met; but he had fought over the same terrain we had patrolled that night and had been ambushed by Vietcong guerillas. Once again I knew whom to thank: He was somebody Lieutenant North had come up with at the last minute.

Gene asked him to tell his story.

"It was about seventy yards from the village of Son Trang 4," he said. "We noticed the village because we'd heard what had happened there."

"What happened to you at about the same spot?"

"Just after we passed Son Trang 4, we were fired on from out of the jungle."

"By what kind of weapon?"

"By an M-60 machine gun."

It was clearly the same bunch that had fired

on us, using the same weapon. As the lance corporal told his story, everything fell into place for the jurors—or so I hoped. Here was proof that such a group actually existed, that they had a machine gun, that they fired on American troops. The lance corporal's killer team had been a little luckier.

"What was the outcome of the exchange?" Gene asked.

"We returned their fire and killed three of them."

"What about the machine gun?"

"We captured it."

"Would you describe it."

"It was a standard M-60 machine gun."

"In other words, an American-made weapon used by our forces?"

"Yes, sir."

I wondered for an instant why Gene was bothering to make the witness state what was obvious to all of us, but then I remembered: the appellate judge. Gene didn't miss a trick.

After a few more questions he turned the witness over to Captain Brown, who hesitated for a moment, then rose to cross-examine. He seemed to be going through the motions now. With no particular zeal he asked, "Did you take any prisoners?"

"No, sir, we didn't," the witness replied. "If there were others in addition to the three we killed, then they got away."

"So you had no real way of knowing whether or not these Vietcong were in any way involved with the earlier incident in which civilians were killed."

"No, sir. There's no way we could tell, but . . ."

"Thank you," interrupted Captain Brown. "No more questions."

Our last witness was one we had counted on from the beginning, though he had flown in only at the last minute, since his testimony was not crucial in establishing precisely what had happened that night. Doctor Hayden Donahue was a fellow Oklahoman and an expert in what became known in World War II as "battle fatigue." In the early 1940s he had worked with veterans in Europe, trying to determine if they should go back into combat or be given time to recuperate. His published studies on the subject were regarded as among the most authoritative in the field. When he took the stand, brushing back his white hair, he looked like a country doctor; but as he recounted his background and publications, you could sense the authority in what he was saying and the way in which he said it.

He told the court that he had not examined me personally because I had been out of combat too long. However, just from reviewing my record, he could draw some reasonable conclusions about my condition at the time of the incident.

"Would you say that your opinion would be beyond dispute?" Gene asked.

"Of course not," he said. "It wouldn't have been beyond dispute if I had seen him that night. But I know what a fighting man's limits are, and they don't change that much from war to war, not if the going really gets rough."

Then he proceeded to describe what happens to a man's thoughts and reactions after he's been in the bush for months, seeing his buddies killed, facing the possibility of his own death with every passing day. He talked about the physical reactions first, then the emotional reactions. And he concluded that after battle fatigue sets in, a fighting man is living at the edge of his nerves, ready to explode emotionally at any moment.

"How would you say a combat veteran acts at such a point?"

"He acts instinctively rather than reasonably."

"And do you think it's possible, given Randy Herrod's time in combat and what he'd been through, that he was suffering from battle fatigue?"

Doctor Donahue nodded.

"Yes, I would say it was more than possible. I would say it was likely."

"Thank you, Doctor Donahue," Gene said, and turned him over to Captain Brown, who chewed on him awhile, but made little headway. Besides, Doctor Donahue had done what he had been brought to do—establish one more avenue of appeal, a reason to mitigate the sentence because of extenuating circumstances. Gene was covering every base.

After Captain Brown had finished and Doctor Donahue had stepped down, Gene rose.

"If it please the court," he said, "we have no other witnesses. The defense rests its case."

At the beginning of the trial, Gene had sent us all over Da Nang looking for a yellow legal pad.

"I've never taken notes in the years I've practiced law," he had said, "but since we're trying a case we're sure to appeal, I'm going to keep

a record along the way—just in case. That way
I'll know what to include in the summation."

So after Donahue had finished and we broke
for lunch, Denny winked at me, then turned to
Gene.

"Well," he said, "it's summation time. Let's
take a look at your notes."

Denny reached across the table, picked up
the yellow pad, and held it up for the rest of our
team to see. On the first page were the words:
TRIAL OF RANDY HE. . . . That was all.

Everybody laughed, and we went to chow
joking about Gene's lack of preparation; but
when he got back in the courtroom, Gene put on
a performance the likes of which few people
have ever witnessed. Speaking for more than
two hours, he went through every item introduced into evidence, every single witness, and
every bit of testimony. He didn't make a mistake
on any of the factual matters, he didn't forget
even a minor detail, and he didn't mispronounce
one of the Vietnamese names used during the
trial. I don't think he could have done better had
he practiced for days.

Brown's summary was briefer, but efficient;
and he didn't hesitate to preach a little, reminding the jury that we had a responsibility to
protect these people whose country we now oc-
cupied. He was a good lawyer and had done his
homework; but he was clearly exhausted, and he
and his teammates had been outclassed. Everyone knew that. The trouble was, such knowledge
could cut both ways, particularly if the seven officers on the jury started to see the trial in terms
of military vs. civilian.

But Lieutenant North had made that viewpoint difficult to maintain. He was the military presence we needed. Besides, Captain Williams had been a significant part of our team. In fact, he was my official counsel, despite the fact that Gene had conducted most of the trial. I tried to remember these things while the judge advocate was charging the jury.

At six o'clock on Saturday evening they retired to deliberate.

It's difficult to explain how I felt at this stage. Instead of experiencing an increased apprehension of what was about to happen, I was relaxed and even elated. I had only one more ordeal to live through—the moment when I would hear myself pronounced guilty and then sentenced to death by firing squad. But none of that would require any effort on my part, except to stand on my two feet, keep my mouth shut, and try not to show any emotion.

Earlier in the trial I hadn't been sure whether or not I could maintain my self-control. Now I could view my case objectively, like one of the reporters in the back of the room; and I believed my defense had been strong enough to win an acquittal in a civilian court, where the Commandant of the Marine Corps could exert no undue influence.

I also felt a growing pride over my defense team. Everyone had performed well: Gene and Denny, Captain Williams, Dick, Harry, and of course Lieutenant North. I even included myself on that list. I had no regrets over the way the trial had been conducted. I couldn't have bought a better defense with a million dollars; and as I watched the seven officers rise to leave the room, I was grateful and confident.

After the last one disappeared through the door, Denny turned to me with a grin.

"There's only one thing to do now," he said, "and I've already bought the whisky."

So all of us—Captain Williams, Gene, Denny, Harry, Dick, Doctor Donahue, Lieutenant North, Lieutenant Ambort, my chaser, and I—went back to the barracks where the civilians were quartered and had a quiet but slightly drunk party. We all drank a little too much because we were letting down after the tensions of the trial, but we were also steeling ourselves against the defeat we were certain was coming. We talked about that prospect for a few minutes, about the appeal and how we would win the case in the end. But even putting the most optimistic face on, we realized that we were talking about grim business, and soon we moved on to more cheerful subjects.

Somebody asked me about my folks back home, and I told them about my grandfather Alvin and also about my Indian grandfather, who had died while I was awaiting trial. Then I made Lieutenant North tell some war stories, which everyone listened to with great interest. Gene and Denny kidded each other about partisan politics, Gene telling stories on the Republicans, Denny trying to top him with tales on the Democrats. Both men were well-known public speakers in Oklahoma, and they put on a great show that night.

Nobody had bothered with chow, and about midnight I realized I was either too drunk or too tired to continue, so I lunged to my feet, started to make a speech, thought better of it, and stumbled out the door. Then I remembered my chaser, who was supposed to deliver me back to the brig. I stuck my head back in the room, called his name, and he came to life on the chair where he'd been sleeping. The last thing I saw was Lieutenant North, a cigar in his mouth, a drink in his hand, cold sober.

My chaser almost ran the jeep off the road several times before we got back to the brig, where he dropped me off, gunned the motor, and then scratched off into the night with a wild scream. The noise didn't help. When I opened the door to step inside the building, I found myself staring straight into the eyes of the duty officer, a captain, who took one look at me and blew his stack.

"You've been drinking, haven't you?"

I started to say something, but thought it would be smarter simply to nod my head.

"Don't you know it's against regulations for prisoners to consume alcoholic beverages?"

I nodded.

"You son of a bitch," he said. "You think you can get away with murder, just because you've got a bunch of civilian lawyers over here. Do you want to go into the Deep Lock?"

I paused, then shook my head.

"Answer me, goddamn it!"

"Sir," I said, "meaning no disrespect, but I'm either going to be in this bastard for the rest of a very short life or I'll be out. Either way, there's not a damn thing you can do about it."

He stared at me for a moment or two, and then I saw his face relax.

"Sergeant," he called over his shoulder, "take this man back to his cell."

I nodded in gratitude, followed the sergeant

back to a minimum security cell, fell onto the bunk, and was asleep before I had time to think about tomorrow.

I woke up to the sound of the chaser, banging on my cell door.

"Wake up, Randy," he shouted. "They've reached a verdict."

I'll say this, as hung over as I was, I was up, dressed, and shaved in five minutes. We drove down to First Marine Headquarters, where Denny met me at the curb with a tumbler filled with six ounces of Scotch.

"Here, boy," he said. "You're going to need this."

I drank it in three gulps, fought to keep it down, took a couple of deep breaths, and in a few minutes I was ready for anything. The whole defense tcam piled into two jeeps and we drove to the judge advocate's building, where we found an empty courtroom. No judge advocate. No prosecutor. No jury.

I turned to Denny.

"Are you sure they reached a verdict?"

"Positive," he said. "The judge advocate himself called. Come on, while we're waiting, I'm going to find out what kind of man you are."

He sat down at the defense table, put his right elbow down on the oak surface, and looked up at me.

"Let's arm wrestle."

I sat down, reasonably confident. I was bigger than he was and a lot younger. But after a second or two, he pressed my arm back onto the table.

"Shoot," he said, "you're no competition. Who's next?"

Gene sat down and tried it, but Denny was too strong for him. Then, as the chaser was taking his seat, the judge advocate and jury walked in, and I snapped to attention.

After everyone was seated, the judge advocate asked the jury, "Have you reached a verdict?"

"We have," said Colonel Blue, his face expressionless.

The judge advocate turned to me.

"Will the defendant please rise and stand before the jury with his military counsel while the verdict is read."

Captain Williams glanced at me, nodded, and we both rose and took our places before the seven men. The Scotch had settled my stomach and calmed my nerves, but it hadn't made me drunk; and when I stood before that bird colonel and watched him pull out the piece of paper, my legs began to wobble. There was nothing in his face or the faces of the others to tell me what was coming.

"We, the members of this court-martial board," he read, "find Lance Corporal Randall Herrod not guilty of all charges and specifications listed herein."

I stood for an instant and tried to think of what that meant. Then suddenly the full meaning flooded into my head like sunshine: "not guilty of all charges." There would be no appeal. No more brig. I was free! I was going home!

I shouted, grabbed up Lieutenant Williams, threw him over my shoulder, and went hooting out of the courtroom. There was a crowd of reporters outside by now; and after I'd put Captain Williams down, they crowded around me, trying to ask me questions. But there were so many faces and so many different questions, I couldn't answer any of them.

My chaser pounded me on the shoulder and then pulled me out of the crowd.

"You gotta go back inside," he shouted.

"You're not my chaser anymore, you son of a bitch," I told him, laughing. "I'm yours." And to prove it, I chased him around the building. As I came back to the front, laughing and breathing hard, I noticed two familiar faces at the edge of the small crowd—Boyd and Krichten. They'd come to see me hauled off to the Deep Lock. Then I noticed Gene, gesturing to me at the front door, and I realized I would have to go back inside.

I walked back up to the table where the board was still seated and threw a salute.

"I'm sorry," I told them. "It's just . . ."

They nodded gravely, still unsmiling.

As I stood there in a daze, the judge advocate ordered that I be set free and then dismissed the court. Immediately there was a lot of handshaking and backslapping among the members of my team, but the judge, jury, and prosecution filed silently out, with not so much as a word. We stood around for maybe five minutes more, congratulating ourselves, and then moved toward the door.

As I stepped out into the sunlight, I saw Boyd and Krichten, still standing at the back of the crowd; and when my eyes met theirs, they looked quickly away.

I thanked everybody who had been part of

the team, two or three times apiece. But when I looked for Lieutenant North, I didn't see him.

"Randy," Gene said, "we're scheduled to fly out of here in less than an hour so we better get moving."

"Civilians get an armed escort," I said. "I'll go with you."

Then I turned to my chaser, took the belted .45 from around his waist, and began to strap it on.

"You won't need this for a while," I said.

As I turned around, I saw two figures running back down the hill as fast as they could move. Boyd and Krichten. Too bad they hadn't waited. I would have shaken their hands. I didn't blame either one of them, wouldn't have blamed them even if I'd been found guilty. They were just a couple of poor rats who had found a way to wriggle out of a trap. I was just glad I had wriggled out too.

After Captain Williams and I had taken the civilians to the airport and returned to his office, I suddenly remembered.

"Where's Lieutenant North?"

"He left early this morning," said Captain Williams, pouring a couple of stiff Scotches. It was noon on Sunday, but both of us knew we would finish Denny's bottle before we got up.

"I wish North had been here to see the end," I said.

"He knew you'd be acquitted," said Captain Williams.

"How did he know that?" I asked.

"Because I told him so," Captain Williams said and laughed loudly.

At that moment the phone rang and he picked up the receiver.

"Captain Williams here."

Then he listened for about fifteen seconds without saying a word.

"Yes, sir," he said finally, "and thank you for calling."

He hung up and smiled at me.

"You know who that was?"

"Who?" I said.

"It was Colonel Millard Blue, the officer who headed your court-martial board."

"No kidding," I said. "What did he say?"

"Let me see if I can remember it exactly. He said, 'I'm not going to tell you how we voted, but I'll tell you this: if we send the little sons of bitches out there, then we sure as hell have to take care of them.'"